RELUCTANT WITNESSES

Johnny Clem, age twelve, 1863 (courtesy of the National Archives)

RELUCTANT WITNESSES

Children's Voices from the Civil War

EMMY E. WERNER

Westview Press
A Member of the Perseus Books Group

Copyright © 1998 by Westview Press, A Member of the Perseus Books Group

Published in 1998 in the United States of America by Westview Press, 5500 Central Avenue, Boulder, Colorado 80301-2877, and in the United Kingdom by Westview Press, 12 Hid's Copse Road, Cumnor Hill, Oxford OX2 9JJ

Library of Congress Cataloging-in-Publication Data
Werner, Emmy E.
    Reluctant witnesses : children's voices from the Civil War / Emmy
E. Werner.
        p.   cm.
    Includes bibliographical references and index.
    ISBN 0-8133-2822-5 (hc.)   ISBN 0-8133-2823-3 (pbk.)
    1. United States—History—Civil War, 1861–1865—Children—
Sources.   2. United States—History—Civil War, 1861–1865—Personal
narratives.   3. Children—United States—History—19th century—
Sources.   I. Title.
E468.9.W47   1998
973.7'083—dc21   97-49387
                                                                                              CIP

The paper used in this publication meets the requirements of the American National Standard for Permanence of Paper for Printed Library Materials Z39.48-1984.

10   9   8   7   6   5   4   3   2   1

For my husband, Stanley Jacobsen,
my friend Ruth Spangler Smith,
and in memory of Mando Dalianis, M.D.,
who cared for the children of the Greek Civil War

CONTENTS

ILLUSTRATIONS

ACKNOWLEDGMENTS
AND CREDITS

Many thanks to Stanley Jacobsen for patiently typing the manuscript of this book and to Rob Williams, Scott Horst, Kristin Milavec, and Michelle Asakawa at Westview Press.

Grateful acknowledgment is made to the following individuals and institutions for permission to reprint excerpts from manuscripts and previously published material:

Adams County Historical Society, Gettysburg, Pennsylvania, for permission to quote from Annie Skelly's "Remembrances of the Battle of Gettysburg."

Atlanta History Center Library/Archives for permission to quote from Carrie Berry's "Diary," Ms. 29F.

Gettysburg National Military Park, U.S. Department of the Interior, National Park Service, for permission to quote from William Hamilton Bayley's "Stories of the Battle."

Indiana University Press for permission to quote from Theodore F. Upson's *With Sherman to the Sea: The Civil War Letters, Diaries, and Reminiscences of Theodore F. Upson*. Copyright 1958 by Indiana University Press, Bloomington, Indiana.

University of Oklahoma Press for permission to quote from Elisha Stockwell's *Private Elisha Stockwell, Jr., Sees the War*. Copyright 1958 by University of Oklahoma Press, Norman, Oklahoma.

PROLOGUE

You my boys . . . know that war is not the fine adventure it is represented to be by novelists and historians, but a dirty bloody mess, unworthy of people who claim to be civilized.

Private George Alphonso Gibbs, Eighteenth Mississippi Infantry Regiment

THE LIBRARY OF CONGRESS in Washington, D.C., is home to three photographs of children taken during the American Civil War. One photo shows a young boy from Ohio, Johnny Clem, who ran away to war before he was ten years old. "He was an expert drummer," wrote his sister, "and being a bright cheery child, soon made his way into the affection of officers and soldiers." Johnny Clem was with a Michigan regiment in all its major battles—from Shiloh to Atlanta—and became a symbol of valor for the North after the press extolled his courage during the retreat of the Union soldiers at Chicamauga.

Armed with a sawed-off musket cut down to his small size, he shot and wounded a Confederate officer who had asked him to surrender. His photo shows him standing straight and proud in his boots and uniform, with the sergeant's stripes he earned for his courage. The Civil War shaped his life: When he retired from the Army in 1915, he was Major General John L. Clem—the last man in the Armed Forces of the United States who had fought in the War to Preserve the Union.

We know nothing about the children who are in the second photograph. They are white Southern refugees, taking to the road: Two boys and a small girl, clutching a doll, sit on a horse-drawn four-wheel cart on which are piled a few chairs, some quilts, and a chest of drawers—the only belongings they would take on their flight. Their mother stands beside the cart, a Bible in her hands. We do not know whether her family found safety with their relatives in the countryside or whether the children ever returned back home.

Perhaps their town looked as devastated as the ruins of Charleston, which forms the backdrop for the third photograph. Four small black boys sit under the one remaining pillar of a stately antebellum mansion and look out onto a desolate street lined by burned-out houses and rubble. It is April 1865—the war has ended, but the desolation and pain it inflicted will last for a long time to come.

The American Civil War was in many ways the prototype of the modern wars we witness today—in Africa, Asia, Europe, Latin America, and the Middle East. Among its casualties, both physical and psychological, were not only millions of adult soldiers in combat but hundreds of thousands of children from the North and South—who were the reluctant witnesses of a conflagration that turned into the bloodiest conflict ever fought on American soil.

Historians estimate that anywhere between 250,000 and 420,000 boy soldiers, many in their early teens or even younger, served in the armies of the Union and the Confederacy between 1861 and 1865. Their experience in battle, seen from their vantage point, bears a striking resemblance to the eyewitness reports of contemporary child soldiers in Angola, Ethiopia, Liberia, Mozambique, Central America, and the Middle East. Some fifteen percent were seriously wounded or died from battle wounds, diarrhea, infections, or malnutrition. Others spent tortured months in prisons like Andersonville, whose conditions resembled the concentration camps of World War II.

In the American West, at the fringes of the Civil War, children and teenagers became helpless victims of massacres. Among them were the youngsters who died in the Great Sioux uprising in Minnesota in August 1862, the underage boys who were executed by Confederate guerrillas in Quantrill's raid on Lawrence, Kansas, in August 1863, and the Arapahoe and Cheyenne children who were killed in the Sand Creek Massacre on November 29, 1864. Their bullet-ridden bodies were scalped and mutilated by Colorado Volunteers in Union uniforms. These orgies of brutality and hate were as ferocious as the "ethnic cleansings" in contemporary wars.

Sherman's march through Georgia and the Carolinas left in its wake a stream of child refugees whose photographs are as heartbreaking as those of contemporary children in flight from civil strife in Bosnia or Chechnya. Other youngsters sought refuge from bombardment by enemy artillery in the caves of Vicksburg and lived on ever-smaller rations of scarce food in cities under siege—in the river towns along the Mississippi, in Georgia and the Carolinas, and in Richmond, Virginia, the capital of the Confederacy.

Northern children were not exempt from the horrors of the war: Those who lived in Washington, D.C., could spot the Confederate artillery pointed at them across the Potomac River and saw the wounded and maimed who filled the hospitals of the nation's capital to overflowing.

On the rolling hills of southern Pennsylvania, the children of Gettysburg would witness a three-day battle that was the bloodiest encounter between the North and South.

Many children on both sides lost fathers and brothers in the bloody conflict. When fathers were absent or dead, lone mothers asked their young sons and daughters to assume responsibilities rarely expected of youngsters today. Children assisted, as best they could, in managing the family farm or plantation and became substitute parents for still younger brothers and sisters.

Much has been written by adult eyewitnesses about the heroism and the horrors of the Civil War, but the voices of the children who were part of that great national drama are seldom heard. The focus of this book is on *their* perspectives of that war—their subjective experiences of the hardships they endured and how they managed to cope with them—drawing, where appropriate, parallels to the experiences of children in contemporary civil strife.

My primary sources are diaries, journals, letters, and reminiscences of some 120 youngsters who were between the ages of four and sixteen when the Civil War began. Boys and girls from the Confederacy and the Union—*both* soldiers and civilians—are about equally represented among the eyewitness accounts in this book. As corroborating evidence I occasionally draw on eyewitness accounts of family members or—in the case of the boy soldiers, on members of their company—who recorded *their* impressions of the children's experiences in their diaries, letters, or memoirs.

The North at the beginning of the Civil War had one of the highest literacy rates in the world. School attendance had become compulsory in the eastern and midwestern states, and some three-fifths of all children between the ages of five and eighteen were attending school on a regular basis. In the South, by contrast, only about one out of five free white children were in public schools, and because it was against the law to teach slave children, few of them could read and write.

On the Union side, boys and girls from midwestern farms and northeastern cities alike left a rich and moving record of what they saw and felt during the war. The voices of the Southern children and the Confederate boy soldiers are equally eloquent, but they come more often from youngsters of the more privileged classes—offspring of plantation owners and professionals who attended private schools or academies, or who had been tutored at home.

The book also includes eyewitness accounts of emancipated slave children. Some joined the Union forces as "contraband soldiers"; others enrolled in schools for freedmen where they were taught to read and write. Some accounts come from slave narratives recorded by the Federal Writer's Project after the war, others from letters of "boy veterans" who served as volunteers with the United States Colored Troops.

Chapter 1 deals with events in 1861: the excitement surrounding the outbreak of war; the enlistment of thousands of boy soldiers in the armies of the Union and the Confederacy; and eyewitness reports of youngsters who witnessed the first shots fired at Fort Sumter, South Carolina, and the first clash between the opposing armies at the Battle of Bull Run, near Manasses Junction in Virginia.

Chapter 2 is based on eyewitness accounts of soldiers from the Union and the Confederacy who saw their first big battles at Shiloh, Sharpsburg, and Fredericksburg and the reactions of their young kinfolk on the "home front" to the high and low tides of victory and defeat.

Chapter 3 captures the voices of former slave children who were emancipated by the Union troops or escaped their masters' plantations. Some joined the Union forces as "colored troops" and distinguished themselves in combat. A few black soldiers who were literate sent letters to their children back home. A fourteen-year old ex-slave from Georgia and volunteers from the New England Freedmen's Aid Society tell us about their days as teachers of emancipated slaves in deserted plantations along the Georgia and South Carolina coast.

Chapter 4 tells of the events in the first half of 1863, as seen through the eyes of young children and teenage soldiers—from the food riots in Richmond to the battle of Chancellorsville and its aftermath. Among them is the eyewitness account of fourteen-year-old Sue Chancellor, who—in three days in May—saw her home turned into a headquarters for the Union troops and then witnessed its destruction by Confederate fire.

Chapter 5 focuses on the eyewitness accounts of children at Gettysburg who saw the three-day battle on July 1–3, 1863, that turned the tide of the Civil War. It also includes the reports of boy soldiers from the North and South who fought the bloody battle to the bitter end.

Youngsters who lived through the siege of Vicksburg from May to July 1863 tell in Chapter 6 of their "cave lives" under enemy bombardment. One of them, young Lucy McRae, was buried alive when an exploding shell collapsed part of the cellar in which she had taken refuge. She was rescued and survived to tell her tale.

Chapter 7 relates the experiences of teenage soldiers in Andersonville, the most infamous prison of the Civil War. Some thirteen thousand Union soldiers died there from starvation, torture, and untreated illnesses and were buried in mass graves. Some of the boy soldiers who spent many months in the pen or prison hospital tell of their experiences and how they managed to survive without their spirits being broken.

Chapter 8 includes eyewitness accounts of Southern children who lived through the battle, siege, and burning of Atlanta in the summer and fall of 1864 and of the boy soldiers from the North who befriended them. Chapter 9 chronicles General Sherman's march through Georgia and the Carolinas in the winter of 1864/65. The voices are those of drummers and fifers who marched with Sherman to the sea, of rag-tag Confederate teenagers in retreat, and of the women and children who bore the brunt of a savage swath of destruction across the heart of the South.

Chapter 10 is based on the accounts of Southern children and of boy soldiers from the Union and Confederacy of events in the closing days of the Civil War—from the fall of Richmond to the triumphant review of Union forces in Washington, D.C. Private Elisha Stockwell, who had joined the Union Army at age fifteen, wrote on April 9, 1865, "We got news that General Lee had surrendered and we lay there all day and celebrated." Young Emily LeConte, whose kinfolk had fought and died for the Confederacy, saw her world collapse that week. "For four years there has been throughout this broad land little else than the anguish of anxiety—the misery over dear ones sacrificed—for *nothing*!" reads her diary entry on April 16, 1865.

The epilogue sums up the major themes that echo through the eyewitness accounts of the children of the Civil War: their astonishing resilience in the face of great adversity and their extraordinary capacity to pick up and mend the pieces of their shattered lives.

Across the ages, the voices of children who were reluctant witnesses to bloody wars speak of courage and despair, of horror and heroism, and of the bonds of family and community and the power of faith that helped them survive. Their tales are told without bitterness or hate, but with a stubborn hope that peace might prevail in the end.

Some eighty years after the end of the American Civil War, on July 15, 1944, fourteen-year-old Anne Frank, in her attic hideout in Amsterdam, wrote:

> *I see the world gradually being turned into a wilderness, I hear the ever approaching thunder, which will destroy us too, I can feel the suffering of millions, and, yet, if I look up into the heavens, I think that it will all come right, that this cruelty too will end, and that peace and tranquility will return again.*[1]

Young Anne died a few months later in Bergen-Belsen—one of the most notorious concentration camps of World War II. For millions of other children in the world today, the nightmare of war is not yet over.

— 1 —

A HOUSE DIVIDED

O N APRIL 2, 1861, FIFTEEN-YEAR-OLD Elizabeth Horton from Mobile, Alabama, wrote to her cousin Emma Barbour, age seventeen, in Cambridgeport, Massachusetts: "Times are indeed troublous, when our city is so flooded with soldiers, thirsting for the blood of those whom they consider their enemies. My fervent prayer is that not a drop of blood may be shed on either side."

Ten days later, on April 12, Confederate troops attacked Fort Sumter. A young Charleston girl saw the "perfect sheet of flame" that followed as battery after battery fired their salvos, making a "rumbling, deadening sound." The Civil War had begun. More than three million Americans would fight in the war, and over six hundred thousand would die in it. Cousin Emma and Cousin Elizabeth, who each had kinfolk in the opposing armies, never resumed their correspondence.

The roar of the cannons in Charleston Harbor woke up the whole country. In Cleveland, Ohio, fifteen-year-old Thomas Galwey was coming from Mass when he heard the news. "I saw bulletins posted everywhere announcing the bombardment of Fort Sumter," he wrote in his journal. "Everyone talked of war."

In neighboring Indiana, fourteen-year-old Theodore Upson was husking corn with his father when a neighbor brought them the news that "the Rebs have fired upon and taken Fort Sumter." Without saying a word, his ashen-faced father went back to their farmhouse. He remembered:

Grandma wanted to know what was the trouble. Father told her and she began to cry, "Oh, my poor children in the South! God knows how they will suffer. . . . Oh, to think that I lived to see the day when Brother should rise against Brother." She and Mother were crying. I lit out for the barn. I do hate to see women cry.

Fourteen-year-old John S. Wise, son of the ex-governor of Virginia and nephew of Union General George Meade, watched when the Stars and Stripes was hauled down from the custom house in his hometown and the state flag was run up in its place.

I had become rampant for war, but never until then had I fully realized that this step involved making the old flag under which I was born . . . henceforth the flag of the enemy. . . . Across the harbor at the Gasport Navy Yard, the United States flag still floated from the garrison flagstaff, and from the ships. . . . Upon those ships, lying there, were many men, who, but a short time before, were welcome visitors at our home. It was almost incredible that they were now, and were to be henceforth, enemies, or that they might at any time open fire upon the town which they had originally come to protect.

But thirteen-year-old T. G. Barker from South Carolina was jubilant. He was at school, bent over his books, when his headmaster entered the classroom and announced: "Fort Sumter has surrendered and is now part of the Confederate States of America." As if shot from a cannon, the boys stood up and cheered, "Hooray! Hooray!"

When word of Fort Sumter's fall reached President Abraham Lincoln in Washington, D.C., he issued a call to the governors of the states and territories to furnish seventy-five thousand volunteers to put down the insurrection. From Maine to Minnesota, from Illinois to New York, men rushed to arms. The Union held that a recruit had to be at least eighteen years old, but thousands of boys in their early and middle teens managed to slip into the army as drummers, fifers, or buglers and enlisted for duty in the infantry and cavalry. Their enthusiasm was contagious.

In Michigan the *Detroit Press* noted on April 18: "The Star Spangled Banner rages most furiously. The national anthem is . . . whistled by juveniles . . . hammered on tin pans by small boys, and we had almost said barked by the dogs." At Shenango, Pennsylvania, young boys organized a "company," elected a thirteen-year-old captain and held weekly drills in the school yard, accompanied by a dinner-bucket drum corps.

Jane Stuart Woolsey wrote from Boston to a friend in Paris on May 10, 1861:

We all have views now [on the war], men, women, and little boys—"children with drums betwixt their thumbs"—from the modestly patriotic citizen who wears a postage stamp on his hat to the woman who walks on Broadway in a "Union bonnet," composed of alternate layers of red, white and blue. . . . So much intense emotion has been crowded into the last two or three weeks that the "time before Sumter" seems to belong to some dim antiquity. It seems as if we never were alive . . . never had a country till now.

There were some twenty-one million people in the North, and just nine million in the Southern Confederacy, among them three and a half million slaves. Between ten and twenty percent of all new recruits who enlisted in both armies were underage and eager to go to war. At the beginning, each side thought the other would collapse within a few months.

Most boys from the North signed up to take part in an exciting adventure that promised reprieve from the boring routines of farm life or school. Others joined the Union Army because they wanted to teach the defiant South a lesson and set the rebels straight. A few, mostly from the Midwest and New England, felt a strong desire to stamp out slavery. When sixteen-year-old Chauncy Cooke left home with the Twenty-fifth Wisconsin Regiment, he was told by his father: "Be true to your country, my boy, and be true to the flag, but before your country or the flag, be true to the slave."

Southern boys sought adventure and glory in the Confederate Army. They joined "to fight the Yankees—all fun and frolic." But they also wanted to defend their homes against an invading army. North or South, the process of enlistment was relatively simple, especially if parents supported the boy's decision to volunteer.

William Bircher was fifteen years old when he ran away from home to the recruiting depot in St. Paul, Minnesota. He was looking for adventure, and he was in a hurry. When informed that he was too young to serve, he returned home and convinced his Swiss-born father that they should join up together. Ulrich Bircher was a farmer and knew how to handle animals. He became a wagoner, and young William became a drummer boy. Father and son were both assigned to the Second Minnesota Volunteer Regiment and served together throughout the entire war. William remembered: "The happiest day of my life was when I put on my blue uniform for the first time and received my drum."

In Texas, sixteen-year-old Albert Blocker signed up as a musician as well, becoming a "boy bugler" in the Third Texas Cavalry. Drummers, fifers, and buglers were considered nonfighting positions, so a recruiter usually allowed a youngster to sign on without worrying about his age. Some twenty thousand boys, like Blocker, served as musicians in the Confederate Army, and over forty thousand drummer boys, like Bircher, served in the Union Army during the Civil War.

Private Harvey Reid in a letter to his brother gave a glimpse of the life of twelve-year-old Johnnie Walker, a drummer boy in the Twenty-second Wisconsin Regiment:

Johnnie is a drummer in the band and when they play at dress parades . . . the ladies see the little soldier-boy [and] always give him apples, cakes or something. . . . When we are marching Johnnie always keeps up with the

*big men, and is always singing and laughing. . . . Everybody in the regi-
ment likes Johnnie because he is a good little boy, is always pleasant and po-
lite and not saucy. . . . His mother sent him a suit of clothes made exactly
like officer's clothes, and Lieutenant Bauman says he will get him a pair of
shoulder straps with silver drum sticks upon them.*

The most famous of the Union drummers was Johnny Clem, who ran
away from home to join the army in May 1861 when he was barely ten
years old. When he offered his services as a drummer to a company commander of the Third Ohio Volunteer Regiment, the captain laughed and
said "he wasn't enlisting infants." Johnny then went to the Twenty-
second Michigan Regiment. "I went along with the regiment just the
same as a drummer boy," he later wrote, "and though not on the muster
roll, drew a soldier's pay of thirteen dollars a month." The officers of the
regiment adopted him as a mascot. Each chipped in to pay his salary and
made sure he had a uniform cut to his size.

A drummer boy's job was to render the calls of reveille, breakfast, assembly, and "tattoo," which later in the war became "taps." When in
camp, the boys might have to play twelve to fifteen times a day, starting at
about five o'clock in the morning. During the day the drummers were
busy providing the beat for marching drills. Other duties included such
tasks as carrying water, rubbing down horses, digging trenches, gathering
wood, cooking, and acting as guards, barbers, or chaplain's assistants.

On the battlefield, the boys communicated orders to the troops, such as
"Charge!" or "Retreat!" Often drummer boys were required to help remove the wounded from the battlefield and to assist the doctors, honing
the surgeon's instruments, removing amputated legs and arms, and
burying the dead. In spite of the heavy responsibilities put on these
young boys, few deserted their posts. Most stuck out their first and even
second terms of enlistment. As the war dragged on, many became old
enough to sign on as regular soldiers.

Many boys, especially tall, strong fifteen- or sixteen-year-olds, found it
surprisingly easy to join regular infantry and cavalry units—an enlistment that would eventually take them into the thick of fighting. On the
evening of April 15, 1861, three days after the fall of Fort Sumter, Thomas
Galwey went to the armory of the Hiberian Guards in Cleveland, Ohio.
"They seemed to like me," wrote he in his diary, "and I liked them. . . .
My name was the first on the company's roll to enlist. I didn't tell them
that I was only fifteen. So I became a soldier."

Fifteen-year-old Elisha Stockwell of Alma, Wisconsin, went to a war
meeting at his little log-house school. He remembered: "When they
called for volunteers, Harrison Maxon (21), Edgar Houghton (16), and
myself put our names down. . . . My father was there and objected to my

Union drummer boy in full uniform (courtesy of the Library of Congress)

going, so they scratched my name out, which humiliated me. . . . My sister . . . called me a little snotty boy, which raised my anger."

Several months later, Elisha devised a new plan to enlist. First, he told his parents he was going to a Sunday dance in town. Then he persuaded the father of one of his friends, a captain in the Union Army, to go with him to a nearby recruitment center:

> *The Captain got me in by lying a little, as I told the recruiting officer I didn't know just how old I was but thought I was eighteen. He didn't measure my height, but called me five feet five inches high. I wasn't that tall two years later when I re-enlisted, but they let it go, so the records show that as my height.*

Down south in Mississippi, sixteen-year-old George Gibbs, beardless and still shy with the girls, enlisted in the Eighteenth Mississippi Infantry Regiment only days after he heard the news of the firing on Fort Sumter. His parents were opposed to secession, and they pleaded with him, saying that he was too young and delicate to go to war. "Nothing would do me but to enlist," he wrote later. "Nothing could shake my resolution to be a soldier." But when the time came to part from his parents, he hid from the other soldiers and had a big cry. "This seemed to help me," he remembered, "and I felt better about leaving home."

Not all Southern youths who enlisted in their mid-teens were dirt-poor farm boys. William H.S. Burgwyn joined the Thirty-Fifth North Carolina Infantry Regiment at age fifteen, after a stint as a cadet at the Hillsboro Military Academy. He was first appointed drillmaster and then promoted to second lieutenant before he turned sixteen. The educated son of a wealthy Southern planter whose mother came from a prominent Boston family, he was accompanied throughout most of the war by a slave who was his servant.

It would take a crash course in drilling and outfitting to make the raw recruits of the Confederate and Union armies ready for war. The North, with its strong industrial base, was in a better position to produce uniforms and weapons. The South, with its cadre of upper-class officers who had attended military academies, including West Point, made better progress in imparting to the young volunteers the rudiments of drill and the rebel yell—"a mingling of Indian whoop and wolf-howl."

Early in the war, recruits would often find themselves marching in their street clothes, and even after both sides adopted standardized uniforms—blue for the Union, gray for the Confederacy—they did not necessarily fit the individual recruit. A sixteen-year-old Union soldier from the Midwest described his first uniform:

> My trousers were too long by three or four inches; the shirt was coarse and unpleasant, too large at the neck and too short elsewhere. The cap was an ungainly bag with pasteboard top and leather visor; while the overcoat made me feel like a little nubbin of corn in a large husk.

Thomas Galwey, after three months of service in Company B, Eighth Ohio Infantry Regiment, wrote: "There was considerable delay in issuing us clothing and equipment. It was not until the second week of July [1861] that we were issued wooden guns, wooden swords and cornstalks with which to drill and mount guard. We went to parade in our shirts, still not being fully uniformed."

As a general rule, the boy soldiers, or "ponies" as they were called, handled the marching drills easily. They were healthy and energetic and often held up better than the older and bigger soldiers in their company. Elisha Stockwell spoke for most young boys in the armies of the North and South: "There were nearly all big men in my company, and one said it was a disgrace to take such little boys as . . . me. . . . But the first hard march we were on I saw him played out and laying beside the road."

Occasionally, complaints were registered with family back home. Chauncy Cooke, who was barely sixteen when he enlisted in the Twenty-

Regiment of young Confederates at drill (courtesy of the Library of Congress)

fifth Wisconsin Infantry, wrote a letter to his mother in which he described his training at a camp outside Madison:

You see my paper don't have the regulation picture on it of Soldiers . . . in battle array. . . . It seems like foolery to the common soldier that for two hours we must stand in a temperature of 30 to 40 degrees [below zero] when we are thousand miles away from the enemy. I had to walk and walk to keep from freezing. . . . The guard house where we sat down between reliefs . . . was little better than out of doors.

The health of our Regiment is none too good. The food we get is to blame for our bad health. The boys threaten a riot every day for the bad beef and spoilt bread issued to us, and all this in our home state of Wisconsin. There is talk that we will [finally] get pay tomorrow. . . . I shall send you a lot of [my] clothing before we leave.

In the opening months of the Civil War, the period of enlisting, outfitting, and training did not last very long—at best two or three months, sometimes only a few weeks. Each side hurried to get troops in the field. Before they marched off to war, both sides gave their young soldiers a rousing send-off. The drummer boy William Bircher wrote from Minnesota:

During the months of August and September, we did post duty at Fort Snelling and drilled a great deal. In October we received orders to proceed

*to Washington to join the army on the Potomac. October 14 we embarked
on steamboats and proceeded down the river to St. Paul, where . . . we
marched through the city. Here we found the streets crowded with people
waving their handkerchiefs. The band played, the flag waived, and the boys
cheered back. . . . As we marched down the river, the sidewalks everywhere
were crowded with . . . boys who wore red, white and blue neckties and fa-
tigue caps [and] with girls who carried flags and flowers. . . . Drawn up in
line, there was scarcely a man, woman, or child in the great crowd around
us but had to pass up for a last good-bye and last "God bless you, boys!"
And so amid cheering and handshaking and flag-waving, the steamboat
came floating down the stream, and we were off, with the band playing the
"Star-Spangled Banner."*

Four months earlier, in June 1861, the boy bugler Albert Blocker had a
similar send-off in Dallas, Texas. His was the first company of Confederate soldiers the town had seen, and their silken banner was the first flag
adopted by the Confederacy. "The people—women, children and men—
old and young—came flocking to the square to see the sight," he later
wrote. "There was shouting, hurrahing and waving of hats and handkerchiefs . . . and an invitation to breakfast that was gladly accepted."

On both sides, North and South, the festive sounds of adoring crowds
would soon give way to long marches along rough and dusty roads. Boys
in both armies would quickly learn that soldiers spend more time marching than fighting. Elisha Stockwell wrote from Wisconsin: "We didn't
know where we were going, as a soldier isn't supposed to know any
more than a mule, but has to obey orders."

Fifteen-year-old Carlton McCarthy, a private in the Richmond How-
itzer Regiment, would have agreed with Elisha. In his *Detailed Minutiae of
Soldier Life in the Army of Northern Virginia* he described the changes that
took place in the Confederate soldiers of 1861 as they hit the road:

*It is amusing to think of the follies of the early part of the war, as illustrated
by the outfits of the volunteers. They were so heavily clad, and so burdened
with all manner of things, that march was a torture, and the wagon trains
were so immense in the proportion to the number of troops, that it would
have been impossible to guard them in an enemy's country. . . . The change
came rapidly. . . . Reduced to the minimum, the private soldier consisted of
one man, one hat, one jacket, one shirt, one pair of pants, one pair of drawers, one pair of shoes, and one pair of socks. His baggage was one blanket,
one rubber blanket, and one haversack. . . . [It] contained smoking tobacco,
and a pipe, a small piece of soap, with temporary additions of apples, per-
simmons, blackberries and other commodities he could pick up on the
march.*

The company property consisted of two or three skillets and frying pans. . . . The infantry-men generally preferred to stick the handle of the frying pan in the barrel of a musket, and so carry it. . . . If, as was sometimes the case, three day rations were issued at one time . . . the troops ate them all if possible. It was not such an undertaking to eat three day rations in one, as frequently none had been issued for more than a day, and when issued were cut down one-half. . . . No soldiers ever marched with less to encumber them, and none marched faster and held out longer. . . . Instead of growling and deserting, they . . . marched cheerfully to meet the well-fed and warmly clad hosts of the enemy.

The North was hesitant to engage the South in a major battle. The first few months were an anxious time in Washington, D.C. Rumors were that some fifteen thousand rebels were already in striking distance of Alexandria, Virginia, and that another eight thousand were near Harper's Ferry in Western Virginia. A few days after the fall of Fort Sumter, the Federal armory at Harper's Ferry was abandoned, but Federal sharpshooters remained in the vicinity on the heights nearby. Virginia forces dismantled the weapons-producing machinery and shipped it south to produce arms for the Confederacy. Less than twenty families stayed in Harper's Ferry and remained "under fire" for most of the war. They lived on the border where the authority of one army ended and the authority of another began; where sometimes the Union forces were in control, sometimes the Confederates, often times neither.

Annie P. Marmion, the daughter of a local physician who remained loyal to the Union, was eight years old at the time. She later wrote: "The great objects in life were to procure something to eat and to keep yourself out of sight by day, and keep your candle light hidden by night; lights of every kind, being regarded as signals to the Rebels, were usually greeted by a volley of guns."

Annie and her family spent a great many nights fully dressed on the first floor of their house and rushed to their cellar during the bombardments, which increased in frequency and intensity during the warm summer months when water became scarce. Often they sheltered runaway slaves and the wounded from the opposing armies. "When will it cease?" was the oft-repeated question asked by the little girl. For that no one had a ready answer. But everyone in Harper's Ferry knew that the war would last longer than ninety days.

The rival capitals of the Union and the Confederacy, separated by only one hundred miles of Virginia countryside, were filling up with troops. In Washington, President Abraham Lincoln declared a blockade of Southern ports. At Warrington Navy Yard in northwest Florida, sixteen-year-old Langdon Leslie Rumph of the First Alabama Volunteers was practicing gunnery to keep Union ships from attacking the coastline. "A few days ago we came near having a fight," he wrote to his father on May 12, 1861. "One man in our squad . . . seemed almost frantic with delight. His countenance was lit up with savage joy when the guns fired."

Thirty-five thousand Confederate troops moved north to defend Virginia against an invasion by Union troops they now daily expected. Fourteen-year-old Benjamin Fleet, who lived at Green Mount Plantation in the Virginia Tidewater region, kept a diary of events. On May 31, 1861, he wrote: "Rode to the academy at Aberdeen but Council did not teach, he broke up, all the boarders have left. I have left maybe never to go to school again. I feel very disconsolowtory & meloncolly. Came home & brought all my books and slate."

Two of Benny's former teachers began to recruit a volunteer rifle company. The day after his return from the University of Virginia in June, his brother Fred joined the company with the rank of a sergeant. On July 4, 1861, Benny noted in his journal, "The most dreary '4th of July' I ever saw, we Southerners will not celebrate it any more but will celebrate the day forever afterward when we whip the Yankees."

Meanwhile, George Alphonso Gibbs of the Eighteenth Mississippi Infantry Regiment had been shipped by train from Jackson, Mississippi, to Lynchburg, Virginia. The long train ride was an eye-opener for the small, delicate boy who had never been away from home. Along the way he acquired a pet rooster, named Kilby. He also fended off the kisses of pretty girls. "This would make the grown soldiers laugh," he wrote, "which would only make me madder. I suffered a great deal from the rough jokes of the soldiers; I learned, however, after a time, to put up with it."

After two pleasant weeks at the foot of the Blue Ridge Mountains, George and his company were loaded into box cars and transported to Manassas Junction, south of Bull Run, where his soldier's life began "in earnest." His pet rooster came along and stayed with him in his tent. "When you called his name, he would run to you," remembered the boy soldier, "and if you were sitting down he would perch on your shoulder." By July 16, some forty thousand Confederates had struck camp near the railroad center of Manassas Junction. Two days later, the volunteer Union army, thirty-seven thousand men strong, marched from Washington south into Virginia. The Federal troops had a good time despite the July heat. "They stopped every moment to pick blueberries or get water," General Irvin McDowell, their commander, remembered. "They were not used to journeys on foot." Hundreds of Washington civilians, armed with binoculars, picnic baskets, and champagne bottles, rode out to see a real battle. The Confederate General Pierre Beauregard had been forewarned that the Union troops were coming. He ordered his men to form an eight-mile line along one side of Bull Run Creek.

McDowell attacked first on Sunday morning, July 21, around 9:00 A.M. Sixteen-year-old Alphonso Gibbs, who had just recovered from a fever, was at the right wing of the Confederate Army. "We could hear the roar of the artillery, the rattle of musketry, and the shouts of the combatants . . . for several hours before we had an opportunity to take part in the battle," he wrote later.

At first, Northern victory seemed so sure that the Union soldiers stopped to gather souvenirs among the rebel troops who had fallen on the field. But holding a hill in the center of the Southern line was General Thomas J. "Stonewall" Jackson. The boy Alphonso was among the Confederate reinforcements that began to arrive in the early afternoon. At one point his comrades thought he had been killed. "A shell struck the ground and burst near me and threw up some rocks; one knocked me down, but I wasn't hurt, and I jumped up and went on," he reported matter-of-factly. He had survived his baptism of fire.

The Union men, most of whom had now been marching and fighting in the brutal summer heat for fourteen hours without food or water, were demoralized when they saw fresh Confederate troops pouring onto the field. The rebels "yelled like furies," one boy soldier remembered. The Union army edged backward; then their retreat became a rout. Some forty-five hundred men were killed, wounded, or captured on both sides in the battle that the North called Bull Run and the South remembered as Manassas.

Two years later, Thomas Galwey of the Eighth Ohio Volunteer Infantry passed over the old battlefield. He observed: "The rains have uncovered many of the shallow graves. Bony knees, long toes, and grinning skulls are to be seen in all directions. In one place I saw a man's boot protruding from the grave . . . leaving the skeleton's toes pointing to a land where there is no war."

After the Battle of Bull Run, President Lincoln signed bills calling for the enlistment of one hundred thousand additional troops to serve for three years instead of three months. Northern morale was at low tide. A proud and defiant South hunkered down for the duration.

At Benjamin Fleet's Green Mount Plantation, as in many other homes in the South, the whole family participated in the military effort. Benny's mother and women kin sewed uniforms and dispatched the first of a great number of boxes of "eatables" to his older brother Fred and his comrades. Little military action occurred that fall in Virginia, and disease became more dangerous than the battlefield. That was true for the Union troops as well.

Throughout the Civil War, more soldiers were felled by sickness and disease than by bullets and artillery shells. Dysentery and diarrhea were the most common diseases, but bronchitis, pneumonia, malaria, diphtheria, typhoid fever, and scurvy were also common. Measles was especially dangerous and killed a great number of the boy soldiers. Crowded together with other soldiers for the first time in their lives, farm boys were especially susceptible to every sort of childhood disease, including mumps.

Benjamin Fleet's father, who was a physician, gave this advice to his older son Fred:

I can't close this letter without giving you another caution about the measles. Whatever you do, don't take cold if possible. Encourage the eruption to come out speedily by drinking freely of hot sage and ginger tea, or sage with extract ginger in it. Bathe your feet in hot water with mustard & salt thrown into it, and when you get over it, for goodness sake, be prudent!

Benny's parents, together with several other families of the Tidewater region, opened their home to soldiers who were ill. On September 1, 1861, Benny wrote in his journal: "Pa & I went in the buggy down yesterday evening to see Uncle Robert who has typhoid fever & Edward went in the wagon after the sick men. Pa had four from the 5th Regiment, North Carolina Volunteers. . . . There were 1150 men in their Regt. & only muster now 200!! All the others are sick."

Two weeks later, on a Sunday evening, he noted: "The sick soldiers have been improving ever since they came up. . . . Pa gave them the medicine every day. They were right well." "Pa" not only took good care of the sick soldiers, he also delivered and christened babies. Imbued with patriotic fervor, he named one little girl "Secessia Beauregard." History does not record if she changed her name after the Civil War was over!

Sixteen-year-old Langdon Rumph did not live through the summer of 1861. His last letter to his father, Dr. James David Rumph, is dated on July 25, 1861. He wrote: "Some two weeks ago I received your kind favor but being stretched out with the measles I could not answer it. . . . There are over 100 with them at the hospital. In all my life I never saw such a sickly time."

Barely three weeks later, on August 14, 1861, one of his friends from camp wrote to Langdon's father:

My dear sir: It is with deep regret that I am compelled to inform you of the death of your son, Langdon . . . which occurred at the hospital yesterday morning. . . . He died a brave boy, and although his life was not given up in the tempest of battle, yet, he & his other deceased comrades truly deserve as much glory as those brave Southerners who fell on the bloody field of Manassas. They died in the service of their Country. . . . Langdon, as I presume you are aware, had been in feeble health for four or five weeks, and had just gotten over a spell of Measles when he was attacked, as his physician said,

with Typhoid Fever, but I think it was a relapse from the Measles, and [he]
died in five days. . . . I have always thought that the prime causes were . . .
the manner in which we are so crowded at this particular camp.

Camp life on both sides was usually primitive and unsanitary, but it
was the only "home away from home" that the boy soldiers knew. When
they were away from the battlefield or drill and had finished their guard
duty, they could do pretty much as they pleased. Many would read
books and illustrated magazines sent from home. Others would keep diaries, write letters, play checkers, chess, or cards, or engage in horse or
footraces. Sometimes, they raced chicken or lice instead. The lice did not
seem to care whether the uniform they settled in was blue or gray. Some
of the "gamblers" were quite young. An Ohio cavalryman reported seeing a fifteen-year-old win $125 in a card game in one session.

Most of the free time the boy soldiers had was spent with a small
group of friends, talking about their loved ones left behind, wondering
how long it would be before they would meet again and when the war
would be over and "peace again pervade their homes."

One of the most popular songs of the Civil War for both sides was
called "Tenting Tonight." Here are the opening lines:

> *We're tenting tonight on the old camp ground,*
> *Give us a song to cheer our weary hearts,*
> *A song of home, and the friends we love so dear.*
> *We've been tenting tonight on the old camp ground,*
> *Thinking of days gone by, of the loved ones at home*
> *That gave us the hand, and the tear that said "good-bye"*

Left behind at home were children who missed fathers who had joined
the Union or Confederate armies. Maria Lewis of Ebensburg, Pennsylvania, was sixteen when her forty-nine-year-old father volunteered for service in the Fortieth Pennsylvania Regiment. He told the recruiting officer
he was only forty-four and signed up for three years. By November 1861,
he had a captaincy. To his daughter he was a hero. She wrote in her first
letter to him on August 13, 1861:

> *As I think for my first beginning I cant find one more worthey than my one*
> *dear Papa I will attempt to scribble a few lins to you to let you know that we*
> *are all well at least as far as helth is conserned. But our minds are never*
> *easy on your account and never will be untill your safe return. Dear Papa it*
> *is so loansome here without you.*

And on September 19, 1861—after a long illness:

I hav nothing to write only that I hope that this dreadful war will soon be over and you will get home safe for o papy should eny thing happen I know it would kill mammy and when I was sick I was so fraid I would die and not get to see you but I am spared and hope to see you again.

Captain Andrew Lewis did not return from the war. He was wounded, captured by the Confederates, and had a leg amputated. He died on July 2, 1862, near Richmond, Virginia.

Ten-year-old Loulie Gilmer was very proud of *her* father, Major Jeremy G. Gilmer of the Confederate Army. One of her letters, written from Savannah, Georgia, survived:

My Dear Dear Father:
   I do want to see you so much. I do miss you so much in the evening when I come in and no one is in, and I am so lonesome by myself and if you were here you would tell me stories and so I would not be lonesome. . . . Write to me what your horse is named. . . . The Yankees have not got near the city yet. The other day some heavy firing was heard and it was them firing into one of our Boats. . . . Mother and Auntee had the headache day before yesterday and they got up yesterday. . . .
   I have no more to say. I am your loving child
   LOULIE GILMER

Major Gilmer was captured near Fort Henry, Tennessee, by Union forces in February 1862. After the "unconditional surrender" of Fort Donelson, he escaped from prison and resumed his service in the Confederate army.

The initial enthusiasm of the military began to cool with the fall and winter weather. The Union army was still smarting from its defeat in Virginia, but the Union navy had made progress in its blockade of Southern harbors. Federal forces captured Fort Hatteras, North Carolina, on August 29 and Port Royal, South Carolina, on November 7, 1861.

As Christmas neared, the soldiers' thoughts turned to their loved ones back home. In the North, sixteen-year-old Charles Goddard from the First Minnesota Regiment left a Christmas message for his younger brother in a December letter written to his widowed mother: "Tell him that he must be a good boy and not trouble his mother as much as I did." In the South, Jessiah Patterson of the Georgia Volunteers wrote to his children from Manassas, Virginia:

I do not know what my little boys and my angel Anna will do for a Santa Claus this Christmas. It would be fine if the little fellows could get up in the morning and find their little stockings full of goodies and cry out, "Sure, it was Pa! Pa is old Santa Claus!" But I don't think we will have such a happy Christmas morning. But it will be hard if the old fellow did not come just because Pa is not at home. Ma would neither kiss nor whip him if she found him in the house filling your little socks with delicacies. I must try and get the old fellow to call and see you, if I am so fortunate as to see him before that time. But he may be afraid of soldiers and keep out of my way.

In churches, North and South, the people prayed for Peace on Earth on Christmas Day.

— 2 —

WAR IS A DIRTY, BLOODY MESS

AS WE LAY THERE AND THE SHELLS were flying over us, my thoughts went back to my home, and I thought what a foolish boy I was to run away to get into such a mess I was in."

It is spring 1862. The words are those of Private Elisha Stockwell, the last survivor of Company I, Fourteenth Wisconsin Volunteers. The place is Shiloh, a little Methodist church located near the west bank of the Tennessee River, a few miles from Tennessee's border with the state of Mississippi. Named for the biblical village whose name means "place of peace," the simple log meeting house would be near the center of one of the bloodiest battles in American history.

In February 1862, the Union armies in the West had taken the war to the Confederacy. General Ulysses Grant and his troops had captured Fort Henry and Fort Donelson in Tennessee, and the Union navy was taking control of the lower portions of the Mississippi River. In the first week of April, Grant had moved some forty-two thousand men to Pittsburg Landing near the Mississippi border.

Elisha Stockwell and a host of other recent recruits with little training and combat experience were among the soldiers under General William Tecumseh Sherman's command who were camping in tents on a hill near Shiloh church when the Confederates unexpectedly attacked on Sunday morning, April 6, 1862, around 9:30 A.M.

Among the rebels was young Henry Morton Stanley, who remembered an incident in the early morning before the attack:

Next to me . . . was a boy of seventeen, Henry Parker. While we stood at ease, he drew some attention to some violets at his feet and said, "It would

*be a good idea to put a few into my cap. Perhaps the Yanks won't shoot me if
they see me wearing such flowers, for they are a sign of peace." Said I "I
will do the same." We . . . arranged the violets in our caps. The men in the
ranks laughed. . . .*

Four out of five men, on both sides, had never been in combat. When
the Confederates attacked, a Union sergeant tried to rally his midwestern
farm boys, "Why, it's just like shooting squirrels, only these squirrels
have guns, that's all." It wasn't that easy! The Sixth Mississippi rushed at
them up the hill. Only one out of four who started up made it to the top.
But the Union soldiers fell back. Only Sherman's presence prevented another rout like Bull Run. Elisha Stockwell's Wisconsin regiment was ordered forward. He later wrote:

*It is very trying to one's nerves to lay under fire and not to be able to do
anything in return. But as soon as we were ordered forward, the fear left
me, and I went forward with a will, certain we would do them up in a hurry
and have this over with.*

The Union troops were still holding in the center—a thin line of farm
boys from Illinois, Iowa, and Wisconsin who crouched behind the thick-
ets that grew along a sunken road. "The brush was so thick," Elisha
Stockwell remembered, "I couldn't see the rebs but loaded and fired at
the smoke until a grape shot came through the tree and knocked me
flat. . . . I thought my [left] arm was gone." But he kept on shooting.

Most of the hard fighting went on in a peach orchard where the Federals lay beneath the blossoming trees, firing at the advancing rebels. Pink
petals rained down on the combatants. "A bullet cut across my right
shoulder," Elisha noted, "and it burned like a red hot iron." Determined
to fight on, the boy took his place in the front line of his company, but his
commanding officer noticed his wounds and sent him back to Pittsburg
Landing, where tents had been set up to treat the battlefield casualties.

Driven back to the river, the Union forces received support from two
gunboats, the *U.S.S. Tyler* and the *U.S.S. Lexington*. Elisha saw some of
the effects of their shells:

*The Rebs had taken possession of a camp that belonged to our troops. . . .
There were four of them playing cards, and all of them were dead. Each had
three cards in his left hand, the other cards lay in the middle of the blanket.
The tent was blown to atoms.*

The gunboats lobbed shells into the Confederate camps throughout the
afternoon and late into the night. The wounded and the dead lay every-

where. Sixteen-year-old John A. Cockerill, a regimental musician who had become separated from his unit, followed in the wake of the attack. He remembered:

> *I passed . . . the corpse of a beautiful boy in gray who lay with his blond curls scattered about his face and his hand folded peacefully across his breast. He was clad in a bright and neat uniform, well garnished with gold, which seemed to tell the story of a loving mother and sisters who had sent their household pet to the field of war. His neat little hat lying beside him bore the number of a Georgia regiment. . . . He was about my age. . . . At the sight of the poor boy's corpse, I burst into a regular boo-hoo and started on.*

Elisha Stockwell, meanwhile, spent the night in a tent full of wounded, waiting to have the bullets removed from his arm and shoulder. He was impressed by the stoicism of a slim fifteen-year-old boy who was sitting opposite him, face down:

> *When the doctor came to him and asked where he was wounded, he looked up but didn't say anything. He was shot just below the left eye and close to the nose. He bent his head over, and put his finger on the back of his neck. The doctor took his knife and cut the ball out and never a whimper out of that boy.*

With nightfall came a heavy rain. On the following day, Union troops regained the upper hand, strengthened by reinforcements that were ferried across from the opposite side of the river. Among them was the drummer boy William Bircher with the Second Minnesota Infantry Regiment. He had heard the cannonading from the distance, but nothing prepared him for the horrible sight he saw when he arrived at Pittsburgh Landing. "Dead men were lying in the mud, mixed up with sacks of grain and government stores," he wrote in his diary on April 7. "Some [were] lying in the water and others trampled entirely out of sight in the deep mud."

This was the first sight of a battlefield for the sixteen-year-old boy: He would never forget its horrors. On the second day of intense fighting, the Union army had finally broken the Confederate resistance and the rebels were withdrawing across the Mississippi border. As William Bircher marched with his fellow Minnesotans up the hill to Shiloh church, where they camped that night, he saw dismounted gun carriages and cannons, dead artillery horses and their dead riders, and wounded soldiers burned alive to a crisp under the fallen limbs of trees whose leaves had been set afire by artillery shells.

On the next day, hastily organized burial details went to work, digging trenches with rude headboards cut with pocket knives: "125 rebels" read one; "35 Union" read another. William Bircher thought of the terrible suffering endured in this place where the dead lay "like grass before a scythe in summer time." He wrote in his diary:

> *How firmly some had grasped their guns, with high, defiant look, and how calm were the countenances of others in their last solemn sleep. I sickened of the dreadful sight. . . . It was too awful to look at any more. Even the rudest and roughest of us were forced to think of . . . the sorrow and tears that would be shed among the mountains of the North and the rice-fields of the far-off South.*

If anyone, North or South, still retained illusions of a short war won by heroic actions, they were shattered by the dreadful reality of Shiloh: One hundred thousand men had fought there; nearly one out of four was a casualty. More than thirteen thousand Union men had been killed, wounded, or captured; the Confederate losses were nearly eleven thousand. More Americans were killed in those two days of fighting than in all the battles of the American Revolution, the War of 1812, and the war with Mexico combined.

The drummer boy Johnny Clem would become the Union's poster child. The smashing of his drum by a Confederate artillery shell at Pittsburgh Landing won him the nickname Johnny Shiloh. In a photograph taken after the battle his innocent, childlike face did not reveal the horrors he had seen. Along with Elisha Stockwell and William Bircher he would march on to other battles, knowing now that the war would not come to a quick and bloodless end.

Two and a half weeks later, on April 25, New Orleans was captured by the Federal fleet under the command of Rear Admiral David Farragut. The South's largest city and busiest port surrendered without firing a shot. But a woman in the French quarter expressed her defiance by leaning out of her window and emptying the contents of her chamber pot over the admiral's head!

During the summer of 1862, Baton Rouge, Louisiana's capital city, came under heavy bombardment by the Federal gunboats that now controlled the southern Mississippi River. On August 6, 1862, one third of the city was reduced to rubble. Twelve-year-old Céline Frémaux, whose father served as engineer in the Confederate army, lived in the city at the time, helping her mother take care of six young children, among them a newborn baby. She remembered:

> *At the time of the bombardment many persons had dug pits, from three to four feet deep, and from seven to ten feet long, and about as wide. In these they crouched in moments of danger and during the battle of August 6th. These pits were now all filled with dead men in . . . [various] . . . states of*

Johnny Clem after the battle of Shiloh (courtesy of the National Archives)

A family combs through the ruins of their home in Baton Rouge, Louisiana (courtesy of the Andrew D. Lyttle Collection, Louisiana and Lower Mississippi Valley Collections, LSU Library, Louisiana State University)

decomposition. When a pit was filled up, an army blanket was stretched atop, the corners held down with bricks, and there ended the disposition of the dead. . . . People were often taken with nausea on the streets. I saw most of these horrors on my way [from school] to our house as I had to cross the heart of the city.

Packing a few belongings, Céline's mother managed to move herself and her children to Port Hudson, Louisiana, where they spent the next five months as refugees in a temporary shelter, taking care of her ailing father. Céline wrote later: "Necessity, humane obligations . . . family pride and patriotism had taken entire possession of my little undersized body. . . . If father could suffer [from dysentery] and do his work, we could suffer and be silent when [we were] cold or hungry or in the dark."

On a freezing December day, all women and children were ordered to leave Port Hudson, for Federal troops were about to besiege the town. Sick with a cold and fever, carrying a small bundle in which were her prized possessions, Céline was on the move again in a military ambulance that carried her and her siblings to Jackson, Louisiana. There she and her family spent the rest of the war as "rufugees"—watching the Yankees come and go.

When conditions were safe, she went to school, learning English and arithmetic from books scavenged from the library of the nearby college, whose students had gone to war. When the Yankees approached and there was fighting nearby, she and the other children would hide in a dark, damp cellar. "Children had become so reasonable in these troubled times," she reported matter-of-factly.

She and her brothers and sisters each wore a strap with a "ticking bag" under their clothes. In moments of danger the family's silver spoons and forks and jewelry were thus distributed, since the Union soldiers were not apt to search little children. Each day, they prayed "for the dead, the wounded and those who loved them," including their father, grandfather, and their oldest brother, who were all now volunteers in the Confederate army. "Children saw some fearsome sights during that awful time," she wrote later.

But there were also some funny little episodes she remembered. Among them was an exchange between a prim and prudish old lady who had relatives fighting in the Second Battle of Bull Run. Céline overheard the following conversation between her and the local doctor:

"Doctor, have you heard anything since the battle?"
"Which battle, Madame?"
"The one lately fought at . . . at . . . er . . . Gentlemen cow's Run, Doctor."

The doctor and bystanders exploded with laughter, and the lady remarked that "there is always a way of chastening words if one is very refined!"

The Second Battle of Bull Run was fought on August 28 and 29, 1862. Led by Stonewall Jackson, the Confederates held their own against the Union troops, hurling rocks at them when their ammunition ran low and turning the battle into a much-needed victory. Twenty-five thousand men were killed, wounded, or missing at Second Bull Run, five times the casualty figures that so horrified the North and South when they fought there a year earlier.

General Robert E. Lee had been placed in command of the Army of Northern Virginia, and his victory had brought him and his troops renown in the Confederacy as well as abroad. But his troops were short on supplies, especially shoes and ammunition. He decided to forage in

Maryland, a slave-holding state in the Union, where many sympathized with the South. In early September, he led some fifty-five thousand men across the Potomac into the southwestern part of the state.

In mid-September Lee set up a defensive line at Sharpsburg, in western Maryland, near Antietam Creek. "Lee's men were the dirtiest . . . I ever saw," wrote a Maryland woman, "a most ragged, lean and hungry set of wolves. Yet there was a dash about them that the Northern men lacked." Another woman observed: "This body of men moving along with no order, their guns carried in every fashion, no two dressed alike. . . . Were *these* the men that had driven back again and again our splendid legions?" Most residents of the small towns through which the Confederates marched stayed fearful behind closed doors.

The Battle of Antietam (or Sharpsburg) took place on September 17, 1862. What follows are the views of three boy soldiers who saw the bloody conflict at different times of the day and from different vantage points: Two were Union soldiers, one was a young second lieutenant in the Confederate army. All three combatants were only sixteen years old at the time; this was their first major engagement.

Corporal Thomas Galwey from the Eighth Ohio Infantry Regiment was in the first part of the battle, which started at 6 A.M. on Lee's left, where Federal troops attacked Confederate forces hidden in two clumps of woods. The Union objective was a plateau on which stood a whitewashed church. Batteries from both sides opened up on the cornfield that separated the two lines. Galwey wrote:

> *Forward we go over fences and through an apple orchard. Now we are close to the enemy. They rise up . . . and pour a deadly fire into us. . . . There is nothing to do but to advance or break into a rout. . . . So we go forward on the run, heads downward as if under a pelting rain. . . . The order is passed along the line for us to charge.*

In the midst of the work of death and destruction that followed, Thomas Galwey found time for an act of mercy. He stooped long enough under fire to give a wounded Southerner a drink of water from his canteen. Next to him lay a Confederate captain with both eyes shot out, still alive and moaning.

By mid-morning, twenty-eight of Galwey's company of thirty-two men had been hit—either killed or severely wounded. "We are now but a handful," he wrote hours later. "The order came to retire. . . . There is only a narrow opening left us. We go at a run, one by one . . . in a terrible gauntlet race. But new men are coming up. . . . As we pass them we give them a cheer and Godspeed."

The battle surged back and forth across the cornfield fifteen times. By 10 A.M., eight thousand men lay dead or wounded. At about the same

*Private Edward W. Spangler, 130th Pennsylvania
Regiment (courtesy Ruth Spangler Smith)*

time, the struggle shifted to the center of Lee's line, a sunken country road that in times of peace had divided one farmer's field from another. Now it was a rifle-pit for two Confederate brigades that were firing at the Union reinforcements.

Among them was sixteen-year-old Private Edward W. Spangler from the 130th Pennsylvania Regiment, who hours earlier had prepared himself for battle by putting forty rounds of ammunition each in his cartridge box and his coat pocket. As he waited for the order to advance he read a chapter from his pocket Bible, while nursing a painfully inflamed leg. He was *determined* to go into battle.

When the order came for Spangler's regiment to advance in mid-morning, they moved so rapidly that Edward, with his stiff leg, could not keep up. He finally managed to join the rest of his unit on the eastern slope of a hill that overlooked the sunken road. "The bullets flew thicker than bees and the shells exploded with a deafening roar," he wrote later. "I thought of home and friends, and felt that I surely would be killed, and how I didn't want to be!"

The fighting was devastating for both sides. Spangler's unit finally moved around the right side and up a hill to a spot where they could shoot down on the road's defenders. The moment Edward Spangler began to discharge his rifle, all his previous fear was gone. The excitement of battle had overtaken the teenage boy. "I hardly noticed the screeching and exploding shells, the whistling bullets and the awful carnage all around me," he remembered.

After he had discharged the eighty cartridges he had carried into battle, he turned over the body of a fallen soldier—the top of whose skull had been shot off—took the remainder of the dead man's cartridges from his box, and continued shooting. The sunken road—now remembered as the Bloody Lane—rapidly filled with bodies. Edward Spangler watched as a Confederate soldier tried to climb over a fence near the embankment and was shot in the rear as he reached the top, his body hanging on the upper rail. "When our regiment buried him . . . he had been riddled with seventeen bullets," he wrote later.

Spangler's Pennsylvania regiment was relieved in the early afternoon after their ammunitions had been exhausted. Only eight of his company—himself and his eighteen-year-old brother Frank included—were unhurt when they left the battlefield.

There was no relief for Second Lieutenant William H.S. Burgwyn, age sixteen, of the Thirty-fifth North Carolina Regiment. He and his company had moved to their positions in the line of battle at three o'clock in the morning. In the late afternoon, they were still dodging "a storm of grape cannister and shells" unleashed by the third wave of Federal troops, which attacked the Confederate right.

At one point in time, when his regiment was about to waiver, the teenage lieutenant caught the colors from the flag bearer and rallied his men, remaining in front of his regiment and cheering them on. "They fired at us all day as hard as they could," he wrote in his diary that night, "and [even] after dark threw some shells. . . . Their batteries were about 300 yards off from us." As night fell, the fighting finally quieted.

September 17, 1862 would become known as "the bloodiest day of the war." The Confederates lost about eleven thousand men, the Union more than twelve thousand. In the evening, Edward Spangler, limping with his stiff leg and blackened from the battle smoke, found the house and barn in which the wounded of his brigade had been collected. He later wrote:

> *The sight of hundreds of prostrate men with serious wounds of every description was appalling. Many to relieve their suffering were impatient for their turn upon the amputation tables, around which were pyramids of severed legs and arms. . . . Many prayed aloud, while others shrieked in the agony and throes of death.*

The next day the wounded of both armies who were still on the battle-field were picked up, and the dead who lay within reach were buried. William Burgwyn wrote: "Just after getting fixed to sleep for the night we were silently and hastily got under arms and took up our line of march to recross the Potomac. . . . The men were completely exhausted."

The Union commander could claim a victory. Lee's attack had been halted, and he had suffered terrible losses. But his army was not destroyed. On December 13, Lieutenant William H.S. Burgwyn of North Carolina and Private Edward Spangler of Pennsylvania would face each other again—this time at Fredericksburg, Virginia. The last battle in the winter of 1862 would be a Confederate victory!

In mid-November, Federal soldiers began their "drive to Richmond," the capitol of the Confederacy. They stopped halfway and made camp on some hills north of the Rappahannock River, across from the town of Fredericksburg. The Confederates took up positions on the opposing heights south of the town. More than one hundred thousand Union soldiers faced some seventy-eight thousand Confederates, separated by the town and river.

The Confederates urged the inhabitants of Fredericksburg to leave town before the Federals attacked it. Six thousand civilians were suddenly homeless. "I never saw a more pitiful procession than they made trudging through the deep snow," wrote a Virginia soldier, "little children tugging along with their doll babies . . . women so old and feeble that they could . . . barely hobble. . . . Some had a Bible and a toothbrush in one hand, a picked chicken and a bag of flour in the other. Where they were going we could not tell, and I doubt if they could."

A resident of the town recounted a mishap that happened to a friend during the exodus:

> *The Northern Army shelled the trains . . . no one was hurt [but] all were panick stricken. Mrs. Barbour boarded the [southbound] train with her children & a featherbed. At Hamilton's Crossing, she got off with her bed, but forgot her three daughters till she found the train had moved on, and for three weeks did not know where they were.*

On December 11, 1862, the Union artillery began to bombard Fredericksburg in earnest, setting much of the city on fire. Many Fredericksburg residents had remained in town, despite the advance warnings of the Union attack. They fled to their cellars. The Federal forces crossed the river on six pontoon bridges under cover of their artillery. They engaged the Confederate defenders in bitter, house-to-house fighting and finally secured the town.

Buck Denman, a sharpshooter from the Army of Northern Virginia, observed the withdrawal of the last Confederates from Fredericksburg. He was behind the corner of a house, taking sight for a last shot when a fair-haired three-year-old girl toddled out of an alley, accompanied by a Newfoundland dog, and gave chase to a big shell that was rolling along the pavement. The little girl clapped her hands in delight, and the big dog snapped and barked furiously at the shell.

Buck's hand dropped from the trigger. "There is a baby," he thought, "amid the hell of shot and shell; and here come the enemy." He grounded his gun, dashed into the alley, swept his right arm around the girl, gained cover again, and with the child clasped to his chest and his musket in the left hand, he trotted up to Marye's Heights, which overlooked the town. The three-year-old girl spent the entire battle with the Confederate artillerymen stationed there and was safely returned to her mother afterward.

In Fredericksburg, Union troops now embarked on a rampage of looting and pillaging. Federal officers detailed guards at the pontoon crossings to confiscate stolen property, but the soldiers managed to smuggle across the river thousands of contraband items, mainly books and other small valuables; one enterprising soldier managed to remove a three-foot equestrian statue as well.

Fifteen-year-old drummer boy Charles W. Bardeen from the First Massachusetts Regiment was on his way to his first battle. Crossing the pontoon bridge into Fredericksburg, he witnessed the sacking of the city: "Stores and private homes alike were plundered," he later wrote, "and what could not be carried was destroyed. Men plunged their bayonets into mirrors, smashed piano keys with musket butts, pitched crockery out of the windows. . . . Got a few relics which I brought back—a flattened bullet and a Confederate bayonet—both of which I threw away on my first long march."

Private Edward Spangler's Pennsylvania regiment entered Fredericksburg on December 12. The battle-hardened teenager was not prepared for an unusual sight that attracted his attention: One of the Confederate defenders of the town was in a standing position, leaning against the corner of a blockhouse with his gun in his hands; the head above his mouth had been taken off by a shell. To regain his composure, Edward took the first drink of whiskey in his life—from a barrel that some members of his company had found among the stored provisions in one of the houses nearby. That night he slept on a mattress and under a featherbed in the town's Methodist church—a luxury he had not experienced since he left his hometown of York, Pennsylvania, four months earlier. In his dreams he saw the headless rebel.

On Saturday, December 13, 1862, around noon, Edward Spangler's division made the initial assault on the range of nearby hills that were covered with Confederate infantry and artillery. "As we came to the slope of the first elevation," he wrote later, "we were met with a . . . frightful fire of shell, grape and musketry. The men [in our hapless division] were stricken down by hundreds."

The left side of Lee's line was anchored on Marye's Heights and on a 1,200-foot-long stone wall at the base of the heights. Edward Spangler's regiment tried to charge the wall and the heights but was shattered by an unremitting blast of deadly fire that pierced the brain of their commander. "Convinced that we had done our full duty . . . we made a bee-line for the city," the boy wrote later.

Fresh troops waited in the streets of Fredericksburg, trying not to look at the mangled and wounded who were brought into the field hospitals that had been hastily set up in deserted houses. Among the reinforcements was sixteen-year-old Theodore Gerrish from the Twentieth Maine Regiment, who went into his first battle that afternoon.

For an hour we lay flat in the mud . . . to escape the shells that were screaming and crashing over our heads. . . . In the midst of all this confusion, our brigade bugle sounded the charge. In a moment's time our men were on their feet charging . . . through gardens, over fences and deep ditches. The air was filled with iron hail. . . . Above us . . . within speaking distance was line after line of earthworks filled with rebels, while above them was the artillery vomiting fire and death incessantly. The ground was covered with guns, blankets, haversacks and canteens, while . . . dead comrades were lying grim and ghastly around us.

Throughout the afternoon, and even after sundown, wave after wave of Union infantry were sent to their slaughter. Around eight o'clock in the evening, the last of the Union brigades were hurled from the field. Night finally brought an end to the butchery. No Union soldier ever reached the stone wall.

Although the Union forces met utter defeat on December 13, they remained on the battlefield, crouched in their forward positions along the ravine, hugging the cold earth. The open plain, carpeted red and blue with fallen Union soldiers, rang out with the cries of the wounded. Richard Kirkland, a teenage sergeant from South Carolina, could not tolerate their agonized pleading. He burdened himself with all the canteens he could manage, scaled the stone wall and brought water to his suffering foes—at peril to his own life. Once his mission became clear, Union riflemen ceased firing, and Kirkland moved from one Yankee soldier to another unharmed—along the front line—on his errand of mercy.

Edward Spangler and the other survivors of his Pennsylvania company spent the night of December 13 in a two-story brick house by the Rappahannock River. In the house at the time was the owner, "a lady of intelligence and good breeding," and her two daughters, ages ten and twelve, "Confederates to the core." At about seven o'clock in the evening, when most of the Pennsylvania soldiers were asleep from sheer exhaustion, a shell penetrated the wall of the house, scattering debris about the room. Edward remembered:

> *My brother Frank was sleeping in a rocking chair near the wall, and my head was on my canteen at his feet. His canteen between the chair and the wall was dinged, and the impact knocked his feet from under him. Fortunately, the fuse of the shell was spent, otherwise there would have been great loss of life in the crowded room. . . . Mrs. Mills . . . and her daughters were in great consternation, when the shell penetrated the wall.*

Theodore Gerrish and his Maine brigade remained trapped on the battlefield that night and all the next day, crouching behind a wall of their dead. The temperature fell below freezing, and a cold wind was blowing across the battlefield. Men now froze as well as bled to death. Finally, at about ten o'clock Sunday evening, under cover of darkness, the survivors fell back to the city. Theodore Gerrish spread his blanket upon a sidewalk and tried to get a little sleep. Later, when the men from Maine buried their dead in shallow graves, the northern lights began to dance in the winter sky. Some Confederates took it as a heavenly sign of their victory.

During the night of December 14, Union drummer boy Charles Bardeen was on six-hour relief duty at a hospital near the battlefield. He attended to eight wounded soldiers, two of whom had gone mad. After his shift was over, he wrote a letter to his mother back in Massachusetts:

> *Dear Mother:*
> *My first battle is over and I saw nearly all of it. . . . Saturday the hardest fighting was done. I saw the Irish Brigade make three charges. They started with full ranks, and I saw them, in less time than it takes to write this, exposed to a galling fire of shot and shell and almost deciminated. . . . I saw wounded men brought in by the hundred and dead men lying stark on the field, and then I saw our army retreat to the very place they started from, a loss incalculable in men, horses, cannon, small arms, knapsacks, and all the implements of war, and I am discouraged. I came out here sanguine as any one, but I have seen enough, and I am satisfied that we never can whip the South. . . . Let any one go into the Hospital where I was and see the scenes that I saw. . . .*

On December 16, around noon, Second Lieutenant William Burgwyn wrote a letter to *his* mother back in North Carolina:

Dear Mother,

The day before yesterday I don't suppose this continent ever has, or will soon, witness such a day's fighting. . . . Musketry came over us so fast that it made a complete tune, and the air seemed as full of minie balls as it ever was of snow or drops of rain. . . . From the commanding position we hold, I see the dead Yankees strewn around where they were in deadly conflict, and the Yankees have not endeavored to bury them. . . . I think because they are evacuating the town . . . they appear to be leaving in great quantities. I never expected to see such a sight.

Fredericksburg changed hands again that day when Southern skirmishers cautiously entered its debris-strewn streets. The town's name was now synonymous with "pillaging" and "futility."

Second Lieutenant Burgwyn found among the battlefield debris an overcoat, a pair of boots, and a cap. They kept him warm during a cloudy, gloomy Christmas. "There was no gaiety in the camp at all," he wrote to his mother. "I was in hope I would get a letter to enliven the day, for a duller Christmas I never wish to be my lot to pass."

The Union lost twelve thousand six hundred men in the futile battle of Fredericksburg. The Confederates lost fifty-three hundred, most of them missing, gone home for the holidays. "Our poppy cock generals," wrote a soldier from Massachusetts, "kill men as Herod killed the innocents."

At Bladensfield Plantation, some fifty miles southeast of the battlefield, ten-year-old Evelyn Ward and her mother had a crowd of young Maryland men as guests. They had come across the lines to join the Southern army.

Evelyn's oldest brother, Will, had been killed in action. "Trying to make things merry for us children and for the Maryland soldiers, Mamma stilled her heartache," Evelyn remembered.

The girls trimmed a Christmas tree with long strings of holly berries and lighted it with nub ends of candles. She and her sisters made little pin cushions for the soldiers, and each one made rag babies for the others. They also made new dresses for their dolls. Evelyn never forgot that Christmas Day:

Mamma had all kinds of little cakes, dried cherries . . . handfuls of chestnuts. . . . With her and the girls taking care of them, the soldiers were merry even though their pin cushions had no pins [they were scarce in those days]. We laughed and talked in spite of the Yankees. I almost forgot to tell that by some hook or crook, the soldiers managed to get a box of real candy for the girls.

The winter of 1862 was passing. Evelyn's brother Charley would soon be eighteen, old enough to go into the army. The war would go on!

— 3 —

THE MAGIC OF
A SCRAP OF WRITING

O N SEPTEMBER 22, 1862, five days after the Union forces had turned back the Confederate army at Sharpsburg, President Lincoln issued his Emancipation Proclamation. It said, in part:

> On the first day of January, the year of our Lord one thousand eight hundred and sixty three, all persons held as slaves within any State, or designated part of a State, the people whereof shall then be in rebellion against the United States, shall be then, thenceforth and forever free.

Some four million African Americans had hoped and waited for their release from bondage since the Civil War began. Young Booker T. Washington, who was only six years old at the time, first became aware that freedom was a possibility when "early one morning . . . I was awakened by my mother kneeling over her children and fervently praying that Lincoln and his armies might be successful." Sitting up late at night with other slave children, the boy would listen attentively to the "whispered discussions" of the adults about the progress of the fighting, which they followed through the "grapevine" telegraph. Some slave children "would go round to the windows and listen to what the white folks would say when they was reading their papers and talking after supper," recalled a young girl from Tennessee. A black woman interviewed as part of the Federal Writers Project remembered:

> I was a young gal, about ten years old, and . . . we hear that Lincoln gonna turn us free. Ol' Missus say there wasn't nothin to it. Then a Yankee soldier told someone . . . that Lincoln done signed the 'Mancipation. Was winter-

time and mighty cold that night, but everybody commenced getting ready
to leave. Didn't care nothin 'bout Missus—was going to the Union lines.

Since the outbreak of the Civil War, thousands of black men, women,
and children had run away to the Union lines, where they were considered "contraband of war." Whether a slave chose to leave his master did
not necessarily depend on how badly he had been treated. Twelve-year-
old Alex Huggins from North Carolina recalled, "Twasn't anythin'
wrong about home that made me run away. I'd heard so much talk 'bout
freedom, I reckon I jus' wanted to try it, and I thought I had to get away
from home to have it."

It was in the "contraband camps" near Washington, D.C., and along
the Atlantic seacoast that excitement about emancipation ran especially
high on New Year's Eve 1862. One former slave who testified that night
remembered the sale of his daughter: "Now no more of that," he said.
"They can't sell my wife and children anymore—bless the Lord."

The Emancipation Proclamation also allowed African Americans, freed
and already free, to join the Union army as soldiers. Some 185,000 black
soldiers enlisted. The bulk of those who entered the army came from the
border states—where enlistment was the quickest route to freedom—and
from the Confederacy. A new all-black regiment, the First South Carolina
Colored Volunteers, joined in an emotional New Year's Day celebration
of freedom at Camp Saxton, on Port Royal Island, South Carolina, on January 1, 1863.

The camp had been established after Union forces had seized parts of
the South Carolina coast in November 1861. When the United States Navy
appeared near the Sea Islands, the plantation owners fled, leaving behind
empty houses, unharvested rice and cotton fields, and thousands of slaves.
Soon after the arrival of Federal troops, Quakers from Philadelphia and
volunteers from the New England Freedmen's Aid Society had come
down from the North to teach the former slaves to read and write. Charlotte Forten, born into a free black family in Philadelphia, had taught in
several New England schools before she came to the Sea Islands. She was
among the more than five thousand men, women, and children who celebrated their freedom there on New Year's Day 1863. "The people were
dressed in their holiday best," she wrote in her journal, "with the gayest of
head-handkerchiefs, the whitest of aprons and the happiest of faces."

Following the reading of the Emancipation Proclamation, the chaplain
presented the regimental flag to Colonel Thomas Wentworth Higginson,
the white commander of the First South Carolina Colored Volunteers. As
he waved the flag, there was a spontaneous outburst of singing. "It
seemed the choked voice of a race at last unloosed," Higginson later
wrote in his memoirs. The song was:

My Country 'tis of Thee,
Sweet Land of Liberty
Of Thee I sing

"It was a glorious day for us all," remembered Susie King, age 15. Young Susie, born in Georgia in 1848 "under the slave law," had been brought up by her maternal grandmother in Savannah. She and her brother learned to read and write from a "free black woman" who was a friend of her family. Susie described in her *Reminiscences of My Life* how they went about their lessons:

> *We went every day about nine o'clock, with our books wrapped in paper to prevent the police or white persons from seeing them. We went in, one at a time, through the gate, into the yard to the kitchen which was the school-room. [Mrs. Woodhouse] had twenty-five or thirty children whom she taught, assisted by her daughter. The neighbors would see us going in sometimes, but they supposed we were there learning trades, as it was the custom to give children a trade of some kind.*

By the time Susie was eleven, her black teacher had taught her all she knew, but then she found a white playmate, Katie O'Connor, who attended a convent school. "One day she told me, if I would promise not to tell her father, she would give me some lessons," Susie wrote. "On my promise not to do so, and getting her mother's consent, she gave me lessons every evening . . . until she was put into the convent permanently." Then the son of Susie's landlord, who was very fond of Susie and her grandmother, gave her additional lessons until he was ordered to the front with the Savannah Volunteer Guards. After the first Battle of Bull Run on July 1861, in which his brother was killed, the boy went over to the Union side because he detested slavery.

When Susie turned fourteen in 1862, her uncle took her with his family of seven to St. Catherine's Island, one of the Georgia Sea Islands near Savannah that had come under Federal control. Under the protection of the Union fleet, she and her relatives were brought on a gunboat to St. Simon's Island, south of St. Catherine's. By chance the commander of the boat learned that Susie could read and write, and the young girl was promptly asked to take charge of a school for the children on the island.

> *I told him that I would gladly do so, if I could have some books. . . . In a week or two I received two large boxes of books and testaments from the North. I had about forty children to teach, besides a number of adults who came to me to read, to read above anything else.*

Charlotte Forten in her article *Life in the Sea Islands* wrote: "I wish some of those persons in the North who say the race is hopelessly and naturally inferior could see the readiness with which these children, so long oppressed and deprived of every privilege, learn and understand." A missionary similarly observed, "They had seen the magic of a scrap of writing sent from a master to an overseer, and they were eager to share such power."

About six hundred ex-slaves were on St. Simon's when fourteen-year-old Susie King labored there as a teacher in her "little school"—the plantation cotton house. The majority were women and children who were afraid to go very far from their quarters. No Union soldiers were stationed on the islands. Susie remembered: "The rebels . . . could steal by [the gunboats along the coast] by the cover of night, and . . . capture any persons venturing out alone and carry them to the mainland." Punishment for a runaway and recaptured slave could be swift and merciless.

Susie was fifteen and newly married when she followed her husband Edward King, a sergeant in the First South Carolina Volunteers, to a camp on Port Royal Island, just outside of the town of Beaufort, South Carolina. Stationed with them was the first Northern Negro regiment, the Fifty-fourth Massachusetts, led by Colonel Robert Gould Shaw, a young abolitionist from Boston. Susie King found herself teaching as much as washing and ironing:

I taught a great many of the comrades . . . to read and write when they were offduty. Nearly all were anxious to learn. My husband taught some also. . . . I was very happy to know my efforts were successful . . . and felt grateful for the appreciation of my services.

One of her admirers, the commander of her husband's regiment, Colonel Thomas Wentworth Higginson, observed that his soldiers' "love of the spelling book" was "perfectly inexhaustible." Young Susie, who held the key to it, was constantly pressed into service. Undaunted, she learned how to cope with the hardships of camp life in a black regiment. Saltbeef and slapjacks were a staple of her diet, served with a pint of tea and five or six hardtacks. Occasionally there was some soup made of dried vegetables. To fend off the dampness and cold of winter nights she would take a mess-pan, put some earth in the bottom, fill it with hot coals from the cook-shed, and put another pan over it. "In this way I was heated and kept very warm in my tent," she remembered. The fifteen-year-old girl was especially proud of a newly acquired skill:

I learned to handle a musket very well while in the regiment, and could shoot straight and often hit the target. I assisted in cleaning the guns and used to fire them off to see if the cartridges were dry, before cleaning and re-loading, each day. I thought this great fun. I also was able to take a gun apart, and put it together again.

Once the troops engaged in combat, Susie took care of wounded soldiers, men who had been cut down in the fighting along the marshy coastlines of Georgia and South Carolina. In July 1863, she became part of the nursing corps for the 54th Massachusetts Volunteers, free blacks from the North, who suffered heavy losses in their gallant assault on the batteries of Fort Wagner, which controlled Charleston Harbor. Susie mourned the heavy losses among "her boys."

Among those who survived were the two sons of Frederick Douglass, one still in his teens, and Sergeant William Carney, who saved the regimental flag and made it back to his line despite bullets in the head, chest, right arm, and leg. Susie nursed him back to health. He would become the first black soldier to win the Congressional Medal of Honor.

Fort Wagner was only a mile from Susie's camp. In the months after the battle, Susie would see many skulls lying about. "Some thought that they were the skulls of our boys; others thought they were the enemy's," she wrote. "They were a gruesome sight, those fleshless heads and grinning jaws, but by this time I had become accustomed to worse things." Later she reflected on her experiences in nursing the wounded:

It is strange how our aversion to suffering is overcome in war—how we are able to see the most sickening sights, such as men with limbs blown off and mangled by the deadly shells, without a shudder; and instead of turning away, how we hurry to assist in alleviating their pain, bind up their wounds, and press cool water to their parched lips, with feelings only of sympathy.

But there were also lighter moments in her life. One of the soldiers on his return from a furlough brought back a little pig, which became the pet of the camp. It was in the special care of the drummer boys, who taught it many tricks. Susie remembered:

So well did they train him that every day at practice and at dress parade, his pigship would march out with [them], keeping perfect time with their music. The drummers would often disturb the devotions by riding this pig into the midst of evening praise meetings, and many were the complaints made to the colonel, but he was always very lenient toward the boys.

Susie King's regiment remained headquartered on the Sea Islands near Charleston for the remainder of the Civil War. While her husband was off engaged in semi-guerrilla warfare along the coast, she was often alone in camp except for the pickets, a few disabled soldiers, and one woman friend. "It was lonesome and sad, now that the boys were gone," she wrote. Yet she soon recovered her sense of humor: "But it did seem now that the men were gone, that every flea in camp had located my tent."

Off and on, after the regiment had engaged in a fight, she would tend to the wounds of the soldiers who were brought back to camp, "some with their legs off, arm gone, foot off, and all kinds of wounds imaginable." She never complained and was disheartened only once when she found herself "cast off to the sea" from a boat on which she had booked passage on Christmas Eve 1864 to visit friends in Beaufort, South Carolina:

> *I remember going down twice. As I rose the second time, I caught hold of the sail and managed to hold fast. Mrs. Walker held on to her child with one hand, while with the other she managed to hold fast to some part of the boat. . . . We shouted as loud as we could. They found us [near midnight], nearly dead from exposure.*

At the close of the war, Susie and her husband returned to Savannah. There, at age seventeen, she opened a private school for black children and gave evening lessons to adults who considered education "the next best thing to liberty."

The Emancipation Proclamation had offered that liberty to black men, women, and children who lived in the Confederacy, but not to slaves in Delaware, Kentucky, Maryland, and Missouri. These four slaveholding states had remained in the Union. There, as in much of the rural South, the life of slave children and their families did not change much during the Civil War, though Federal troops would occasionally offer fugitive slaves shelter and protection.

Fifteen-year-old Mattie Jackson and her mother worked as slaves for the Lewis family of St. Louis, Missouri, when the Civil War broke out. In her autobiography *The Story of Mattie J. Jackson,* written shortly after the war had ended, Mattie told of what happened when the Union army took over a Confederate camp and set up their headquarters nearby.

> *My mother and myself could read enough to make out the news in the papers. The Union soldiers took much delight in tossing a paper over the fence to us. It aggravated my mistress very much. My mother used to sit up nights and read to keep posted about the war. . . . On one occasion Mr. Lewis searched my mother's room and found a picture of President Lincoln, cut from a newspaper, hanging in her room. He asked her what she was doing with old Lincoln's picture. She replied it was there because she liked it. He then knocked her down three times.*

Mattie and her mother were not easily intimidated: "The days of sadness for mistress—who worried that Niggers and Yankees were seeking to take over the country—were days of joy for us," she wrote. Mattie finally ran away from the Lewis household, seeking protection at the Union arsenal, because she had been severely beaten for being "saucy." Her mother, seeing the severe head wound that had been inflicted on Mattie, bid her daughter to go with her blessings. Mattie gained admission to the Adjutant's Office:

When the [Union] General found I was there he sent me to a boarding house. I remained there three weeks . . . I wore the same stained clothing as when I was so severely punished which had left a mark on my head which will ever remind me of my treatment in slavery.

After three weeks Mr. Lewis came to get the girl. Disobeying the order of the Union general "to take her home and treat her right," he put Mattie in the trader yard, where slaves were held until they were auctioned off. She was confined there for three months until the general was alerted by his cook that Lewis had disobeyed his orders. The man was arrested, given one hundred lashes, and ordered to pay a $3,000 fine. Mattie was let out of confinement, but now her angry master abused her and her family even more.

In March 1863, some ten weeks after the Emancipation Proclamation had come into effect in the Confederacy, Mattie, her mother, and a younger brother and sister were kidnapped by a riverboat captain and sold into slavery in Lexington, Kentucky, another slaveholding state that had not seceded from the Union.

We were all sold for extravagant prices. The Captain paid eight hundred dollars for my mother and my [six-year-old] brother. My sister, age sixteen, was sold for eight hundred and fifty dollars; I was sold for nine hundred dollars. This was in 1863. . . . I was not allowed enough to eat, exposed to the cold, and not allowed through the cold winter to thoroughly warm myself. . . . I was constantly kept at work of the heaviest kind . . . compelled to wash till ten and twelve o'clock at night. There were three deaths in the family while I remained there and the entire burden was put upon me. . . . I was then seventeen years of age.

For six months, Mattie plotted her escape. She would rise early in the morning to make contacts with "colored people" who assisted slaves to escape by the Underground Railroad. She finally succeeded by pretending to go to church one Sunday morning when her mistress went out for a ride.

I had attached my whole wardrobe [under my hoopskirt] by a cord around my waist. . . . I had nine pieces of clothing concealed on my person and as the string which fastened them was small, it caused me considerable discomfort. To my great satisfaction my master and mistress drove down the street in great haste and were soon out of sight. I saw my guide patiently awaiting me. I followed him at a distance until we arrived at the church, and there met two young ladies, one of whom handed me a pass. . . . There was a company of soldiers about to take passage across the ferry [on the Ohio]. . . . I followed, showed my pass and proceeded up the stairs of the boat. While ascending . . . the cord which held my bundle of clothing broke, and my feet became entangled in my wardrobe, but by proceeding, the first step released one foot and the next the other. . . . I seated myself in a remote corner of the boat, and in a few moments I landed on free soil for the first time in my life.

In Jefferson City, Mattie took a train to Indianapolis and found a boarding house and a place of service of her own choice. Then she set about to improve her education: "I could read a little, but was not allowed to learn [to write] in slavery. I was obliged to pay twenty-five cents for every letter written for me. I now began to feel that as I was free, I could learn to write as well as others." Her landlady volunteered to teach her, and she could not have found a more willing pupil.

One of the more dramatic changes that took place in slave families during the Civil War was the military service of fathers in the Union army. No matter how humble their rank and pay, as soldiers they could take on the role of defenders of their children and their liberty. One letter that has survived in the records of the Sixty-seventh United States Colored Infantry Regiment was written by Private Spotswood Rice to his daughters Mary and Caroline. Rice, an ex-slave from Missouri, was in the military hospital in St. Louis with chronic rheumatism when he took pen in hand to write to his children. He had just learned that Kitty Diggs, the woman who owned his daughter Mary, prohibited her from visiting him and accused him of trying to "steal" the child:

My children. I take my pen in had to rite you a few lines to let you know that I have not forgot you and that I want to see you as bad as ever. . . . Don't be uneasy my children. I expect to have you. If Diggs don't give you up this Government will and I feel confident that I will get you. Your Miss Kitty said that I tried to steal you. But I'll let her know that god never intended for man to steal his own flesh and blood. . . . I once thought that I had some respect for them but now my respect is worn out and I have no sympathy for slaveholders. And as for her cristianantty I expect the Devil has Such in hell.

To make sure that "Miss Kitty" got the message, Private Spotswood Rice dispatched another letter directly to her on the same day:

> *I received a letter from Cariline telling me that you say I tried to steal . . . my child away from you. Now I want you to understand that mary is my Child, and she is a God given rite of my own and you may hold on to her as long as you can but I want you to remember this one thing that the longer you keep my child from me the longer you will have to burn in hell. Now you call my children your property not so with me my Children is my own and I expect to get them and when I get ready to come after mary I will have bout a power and autherity to bring her way to execute vengencens on them that holds my Child. I have no fear about getting mary out of your hands this government gives cheer to me and you cannot help your self.*

A thousand black troops would be coming through her town, Rice warned the woman, and when they did, he would get his children back. In his letter to his daughters he added eight hundred white troops for good measure. Rice eventually succeeded in reuniting his family.

Others were not as fortunate. Amie Lumpkin, an ex-slave from South Carolina, remembered what happened to her family after her father joined the Union forces:

> *My daddy go' way to de war 'bout this time, and my mammy and me stay in our cabin alone. She cry and wonder where he be, if he is well, or he be killed, and one day we hear he is dead. My Mammy, too, pass in a short time.*

To escape vengeful slave owners, black women and children would often go along with their men to the recruitment centers or leave on their own at some later point, settling near army camps where their husbands, fathers, or sons were stationed. Military officials were quite unprepared for them, and even the most considerate officers did not give much thought to their welfare. Captain Hiram Cornell, stationed at Fulton, Missouri, wrote a letter to the Provost Marshall General of the Department of Missouri asking for guidance:

> *Colonel. The wife of a colored recruit came into my Office the other night and says she has been severely beaten and driven from home by her master and owner. She has a child some two years old with her, and says she left two larger ones at home. She desires to be sent forward with her husband; says she is willing to work and expects to do so at home or elsewhere, as her master told her never to return to him; that he could not, and would not support the woman. What is proper for me to do in such cases?* What are we to do with the women and children?

Contraband Jackson, a servant in the Confederate army (courtesy of the Massachusetts Commandery, Military Order of the Loyal Legion and U.S. Army Military History Institute)

Home for the black families who followed their men to military camps was often a cast-off tent, an abandoned shed, or a flimsy shack built out of branches. Women cooked in the open air, buying or bartering from sutlers who came into army camps to sell provisions. Latrines were holes in the ground. Some of the families got free blankets and clothing from Northern missionaries. The older children did whatever kind of work they could find—cooking, cleaning, doing laundry for the officers, and caring for the wounded.

Young boys accompanied the army to the field, serving as drummer boys or personal servants for officers. Some of them were killed or wounded. Sergeant Isaac Wood was with the Forty-first U.S. Colored Infantry Regiment at Fort Harrison, Virginia, when he met a twelve-year-old boy in the hospital. He was so impressed by the youngster's fortitude that he wrote a letter to the *Christian Recorder*, a weekly newspaper that reported on the experiences of black soldiers during the Civil War:

While passing through one of the hospital wards recently, I caught the eye of a little colored boy, who looked just as if he desired to speak to me. So I went over to him, and said:

"Well, my little fellow, what is the trouble with you?"

"Oh, no trouble sir; only I've lost a leg."

"Why, you are a young hero, to shoulder a musket."

"I wasn't a soldier, sir; I was the Captain's waiter."

"Well, how did you come, then, to get in the way of a ball?"

"I didn't sir, it got in my way. I wanted to let it pass, but it wouldn't and so it took my leg off."

"What are you going to do when you get well?"

"Going back to the Captain, sir; he will take care of me."

Written correspondence between black soldiers whose families remained under the control of slave owners was difficult. Unlike Private Spotswood Rice and Sergeant Isaac Wood, most could not read and write. But the men could usually turn to an army chaplain or a volunteer in the camp who was willing to read and write letters for the soldiers. Wives and children at the receiving end had a harder time. Only those who had a literate friend or kin or who knew a neighbor who was a Union sympathizer could correspond. Ann Valentine, a slave from Missouri, searched for two weeks to find someone who could read a letter sent to her by her soldier husband. A white, non-slaveholding neighbor who heard about her plight finally offered to read the letters and write back. He included a note of warning for the husband: "Andy, if you send me any more letters for your wife . . . direct them plainly to James A. Carney, Paris, Monroe County, MO. . . . If you send any money I will give that to her myself." Ann told her husband through her correspondent:

Drummer Jackson, Seventy-ninth U.S. Colored Troops (courtesy of the Massachusetts Commandery, Military Order of the Loyal Legion and the U.S. Army Military History Institute)

They are treating me worse and worse every day. Our child cries for you. Send me some money as soon as you can for me and my child are almost naked. . . . Do not send any of your letters to Hogsen [the slave owner] especially those having money in them as he will keep the money. Do the best you can and do not fret too much for me for it won't be long before I will be free.

Ann had to wait a while. It would take two more years of bitter fighting and much suffering before jubilant black men, women, and children could sing, "Slavery chain done broke at last." Meanwhile some thirty-eight thousand black soldiers and nearly a thousand black sailors would give their lives for their "sweet land of liberty."

— 4 —

THE MEN HAD
ALL GONE TO WAR

NEW YEAR'S DAY 1863 PROMISED FREEDOM to the slaves, but no end to the war between the North and South. In the Confederacy, food and other necessities of life had become scarce; the blockade of Southern ports by the Union navy was beginning to take its toll on civilians and soldiers alike.

Ten-year-old Evelyn Ward at Bladensfield, Virginia, remembered: "About this time supplies began to be very scarce. There were no sugar or coffee or tea, no new calicos or cotton. There were no men to keep the stores . . . they had all gone to the War." But her parents found ways of making the limited supplies last as long as possible. Wrote the little girl:

> Mother . . . had rye toasted with just enough coffee to flavor it to make the coffee hold out. Father planted a big patch of sorghum. . . . Mr. Mothershead . . . got a mill to grind it and boil the juice down to make molasses. . . . It made fine molasses, and Sylvia made good gingerbread with it. When all the candies were gone from the stores, we made taffy of sorghum, and after the . . . nights had become frosty, we used to cut down a sorghum cane, peel off a joint, and chew the pith.

The food shortage was beginning to reach from the countryside into the Southern towns and cities. In Richmond a government clerk noted in his journal:

> Some idea may be formed of the scarcity of food in this city from the fact that while my youngest daughter was in the kitchen today, a young rat came out of its hole and seemed to beg for something to eat; she held out

some bread which it ate from her hand and seemed grateful. Several others soon appeared and were as tame as kittens. Perhaps we shall have to eat them.

Many refugees from Fredericksburg had fled to Richmond during the bombardment. Among them were Betty Herndon Maury and her five-year-old daughter, Nanny Belle. "She is the most singular nervous child I ever saw," Betty Maury wrote in her diary on January 27, 1863. "A band of music is perfect terror to her. She shrieks from going out, and is afraid to go to sleep for fear of dreaming bad dreams. . . . I see more and more plainly every day by how slender a thread her life hangs." Eight months pregnant, Betty Maury faced eviction from her rented lodgings, as Richmond was being crowded to excess by refugees from the countryside.

She was not alone. Judith McGuire, another well-born refugee and a close friend of General Lee and his family, trudged the streets of Richmond for weeks searching for a room. She met a young war widow with three children who had fled Fredericksburg during the winter. The widow could not find enough work to support her children, so a neighbor provided her with a room rent-free. A scrubby garden plot yielded some turnip tops, which she boiled and fed to the children. When Judith asked if this satisfied their hunger, the gaunt refugee answered:

Well, it is something to go upon for a while, but it does not stick by us like bread does, and then we gets hungry again, and I am afraid to let the children eat them too often, lest they should get sick; so I tries to get them to go to sleep; and sometimes the woman in the next room will bring the children her leavings, but she is monstrous poor.

As the Northern blockade held, prices in the Confederacy continued to rise at the rate of ten percent a month. Scarcity made Southern women inventive. They made needles from hawthorn brushes, paint brushes from hog bristles, rope from Spanish moss, red dye from figs, and tea from raspberry leaves. They substituted coffee with ground acorns, beets, chicory, corn, okra, peas, and pumpkin seeds—"all that is wanted is something to color the water."

Said a young Richmond girl: "We are starving. As soon as enough of us get together we are going to take the bakeries and each of us will take a loaf of bread. That is little enough for the government to give us after it has taken all our men."

On April 2, 1863, nearly a thousand women and children in Richmond banded together and "marched along silently and in order." They methodically emptied stores of goods and ignored the pleading of the mayor and the presence of Confederate troops. In desperation, Confeder-

Departure from Fredericksburg, Virginia, before the bombardment (courtesy of the Gettysburg National Military Park)

ate President Jefferson Davis appeared and spoke with "great kindness and sympathy." The women moved on, taking their food with them. Over forty-eight hours later, an observer noted, "Women and children are still standing in the streets, demanding food." Similar incidents took place in the capital cities of Alabama and Georgia and in North and South Carolina.

Many Southern colleges and universities shut their doors, as did many country schools because teachers and students were off to the war. The most endangered were the public secondary schools. For those schools that stayed open, there was mounting pressure for a curriculum and textbooks that were biased in favor of the Confederacy. Textbooks supplied by Northern publishers were discarded, and new ones were hastily written. An elementary arithmetic book popular in the South posed the question, "If one Confederate soldier kills 90 Yankees, how many Yankees can 10 Confederate soldiers kill?"

The Geographical Reader for the Dixie Children, written by Mrs. Marinda B. Moore and published in 1863 in Raleigh, North Carolina, gave this Confederate perspective on the origins of the War Between the States:

Return to Fredericksburg after the battle (courtesy of the Gettysburg National Military Park)

In the year 1860, the Abolitionists became strong enough to elect one of their men for President. Abraham Lincoln was a weak man, and the South believed he would allow laws to be made, which would deprive them of their rights. So the Southern States seceded, and elected Jefferson Davis for their President. This so enraged President Lincoln that he declared war, and has exhausted nearly all the strength of the nation, in a vain attempt to whip the South back into the Union. Thousands of lives have been lost, and the earth has been drenched with blood; but still Abraham is unable to conquer the "Rebels" as he calls the South. The South only asked to be let alone, and to divide the public property equally. It would have been wise of the North to have said to her Southern sisters, "If you are not content to dwell with us any longer, depart in peace."

At Bladensfield, young Evelyn Ward listened to the news that her parents read aloud from the Richmond papers. "The lists of the killed and wounded were always read [first]," she remembered. Her brother Will had already died in action in 1862; her brother Charley would be another battlefield casualty a year later. Cousin Philip Lewis was killed as well. By the time the Civil War had reached its midpoint, every white Southern family, rich or poor, had a brother, cousin, father, or uncle who had gone off to war and been killed or wounded. Virtually every day's casualty list contained the names of relatives or friends.

Still, the people of the Confederacy carried on. "We felt thrilled through and through by the accounts of the brave fighting our dear people were doing," wrote Evelyn Ward. "We children were always drilling, marching, fighting—the whites as officers in the front rank, the blacks coming behind. The cows were the Yankees, and I am afraid we didn't always drive them as slowly as Father wanted."

The road in front of Green Mount Plantation, the home of Benny Fleet, was busy with soldiers and supply trains. Benny's mother gave her scarce provisions freely to the men and their mounts, sometimes to as many as ten a day. In April 1863, she wrote to her soldier son Fred, "I want my children to remember when we are dead and gone, that their parents . . . gave with free hand." Benny went back to school but confessed in his diary, "We have studied very little." There were constant rumors of invasions. At Green Mount the "1001st report of Yankees coming . . . went in one ear and came out the other."

But the Yankees did come in full force—late in April 1863. They crossed the Rapahannock River, nine miles west of Fredericksburg, in an effort to surprise General Lee. On April 30, General Joseph Hooker reached Chancellorsville and made his headquarters in Chancellor House, a large plantation home surrounded by slave quarters. At the time of Hooker's arrival, it was occupied by Mrs. Chancellor, six of her daughters, and her "half-grown" son. Sue Chancellor, who was fourteen at the time, remembered how they secreted their valuables: "We put on all the clothes we could, and my sisters took spoons and forks and pieces of the silver tea service . . . and fastened them securely in their hoop skirts."

When General Hooker arrived, the Chancellor family was ordered to move into one of the back rooms of the house. There they were joined by neighbors who fled to or were brought to the house for refuge, until there were sixteen women and children in one crowded room, sleeping on pallets on the floor. "We heard cannon fire," Sue remembered. "We knew that the troops were cutting down trees and throwing up breastworks. . . . They . . . seemed to be very confident of victory."

But Hooker could not fool Lee. At a midnight "cracker barrel" conference between Lee and Major General Stonewall Jackson on May 1, Lee decided to send Jackson's men twelve miles past the Union front and around it to its weakest spot. When the Confederates attacked at 5:15 in the evening on May 2, the Union soldiers, lounging in camp, were playing cards, their rifles stacked.

A member of Jackson's brigade remembered: "We ran through the enemy's camps. . . . Tents were standing and camp-kettles were on fire, full of meat. I saw a big Newfoundland dog, lying in one tent as if nothing had happened. We had a nice chance to plunder . . . and search the dead, but the men were afraid to stop, as they had to keep up with the artillery."

Fifteen-year-old Charles Bardeen, drummer boy with the First Massachusetts Regiment, noted in his diary that night: "The 11th Corps broke and our Corps had to take their place. The fighting was terrific all night." 'Sixteen-year-old Ed Spangler's regiment was a short distance away from Chancellorsville when the disaster began. "Shortly after," he remembered, "we encountered stampeded wagons, ambulances, packmules, cannon and caissons, with men and horses running for their lives."

Spangler's Pennsylvania regiment was ordered to stay the Confederate advance and arrest the rout. He later wrote:

> *It was the most frightful and terrible night I ever experienced. . . . The opposing lines in many places in the total darkness and thickets of the woods ran against each other at haphazard; disorder reigned supreme among the intermingled contestants and the din was appalling. In the fitful intervals of fire arose the groans of the wounded. . . . Finally, about 2 A.M., from sheer exhaustion, the combat languished, and finally died away—the forest strewn with the dead and wounded.*

Sixteen-year-old Henry Clay Rooney was among the Georgia Volunteers who fought against the Pennsylvanians: "Heavy artillery was in action . . . and we were subjected to a continuous and galling fire of grapeshot and canister, and so severe was this, it tore away the bark of the trees," wrote he later. "In the midst of this inferno a brave officer of my company, near me, was struck by a grapeshot, cutting off both legs and throwing his flesh into a nearby tree."

On May 3 the drummer boy Bardeen wrote—with a touch of gallow's humor—"Baxter and Badger of my Company were killed. Glad that they weren't taking us alphabetically: I should have been between them. We finally fell back to the rear of the Chancellorsville house." While General Hooker watched the fighting from the porch of the Chancellor House, a Confederate shell split the pillar against which he was leaning and knocked him unconscious.

Sue Chancellor and her family had been taken to the basement of their house when the fighting grew fierce. "The house was full of the wounded," the girl remembered. "They had taken our sitting room as an operating room, and our piano served as an amputating table. One of the surgeons came to my mother and said 'There are two wounded rebels here and if you like, you can attend to them' and she did. . . . The surgeons brought my mother a bottle of whiskey and told her that she must take some and so must we all. We did. . . . Upstairs they were bringing in the wounded, and we could hear their screams of pain."

Early next morning, the sixteen women and children were brought up from the basement. In passing the upper porch, Sue could see the chairs ridden with bullets, piles of legs and arms outside of the sitting room window, and rows of dead bodies covered with canvas. The house suddenly caught on fire (presumably from a cannon shell or bomb), and the terrified band of women and children stumbled out of the building as its pillars collapsed:

Slowly we picked our way over the bleeding bodies of the dead and wounded—[Union] General Dickinson riding ahead, mother with her hand on his knee, I clinging close to her, and the others following behind. At our last look, our old home was completely enveloped in flames. Mother, a widow with six dependent daughters, and her all was destroyed.

The Chancellor family found a refuge across the river in the Federal lines, where they were kept under guard for ten days. Sue Chancellor fondly remembered a little Union drummer boy named Thacker who assisted her sister, who had fainted after their long odyssey: "He got some ice and a lemon for sister and took his clean bandanna handkerchief and tied up her head. He said 'If this is on to Richmond, I want none of it. I would not like to see my mother and sister in such a fix.'"

Meanwhile in the thick tangle of woods around Chancellorsville, the brush had caught fire, trapping large numbers of the wounded from both sides. One Union man described what he saw:

I was working away, pulling out Johnnies [Johnny Rebels] and Yanks, when one of the wounded Johnnies . . . toddled up and began to help. . . . We were trying to rescue a young fellow in gray. The fire was all around him. The last I saw of that fellow was his face. . . . His eyes were big and blue, and the hair like raw silk surrounded by a wreath of fire. . . . I heard him scream, "O, Mother! O, God!". . . . After it was over . . . me and them rebs tried to shake hands.

On May 4, drummer boy Bardeen noted in his diary, "Some slight attempts were made during the day but no regular fighting." His diary entry the next day read, "Orders to retreat were received to our great surprise and the whole army recrossed the river." The Union defeat was total.

Hooker's army had more than seventeen thousand casualties; the Confederates lost thirteen thousand of their men, among them Stonewall Jackson, who died from a wound received under "friendly fire." The South mourned his loss. Wrote Benny Fleet's brother Fred to his father at Green Mount: "Oh! How sad it was to hear of the death of the noble and good General Jackson! The victory our brave troops gained at Chancellorsville was no victory with so severe a loss."

Lee followed up his victory with a bold stroke. He invaded the Union once more, first moving into the Blue Ridge Mountains, then north into western Virginia, and on to Pennsylvania. He hoped to strike a decisive blow against the North. The children on the plantations of northern Virginia whose brothers marched in Lee's army were cheering all the way.

"Glorious news" scribbled Benny Fleet in his journal. "Our Army is in Pennsylvania." In the diary eleven-year-old Katie Darling Wallace of Glencoe, Virginia, began on July 5, 1863, she wrote: "I think our people did right to invade the enemy's country. It's the only way to bring them to their right senses. I wonder where my dear Brothers are to-night?"

— 5 —

IT SEEMS LIKE SOME
FEARFUL DREAM

ON JULY 17, 1863—two weeks after the battle that turned the tide of the Civil War—a young girl from Gettysburg, Pennsylvania, wrote a letter to her cousin in Indiana:

> *My dear Mina:*
> *Your request that I should tell you 'all that I have passed through,' I am afraid I cannot comply with, for I have* lived *a lifetime in the past few weeks, and yet, to look back, it seems like some fearful dream. God grant that you, that none I love, may ever pass through such scenes, or witness such bloody, fearful sights! Words can give you no conception. It was perfect agony. . . . If the Rebels are going to invade your State, as they have this, I would advise you to pack up and go as far north as you can. Your affectionate cousin,*
> *Annie Young*

Before the Battle

A month earlier, in June 1863, there had been rumors that Confederate troops were crossing into southern Pennsylvania, but few people in Gettysburg believed that the rebels would come to their sleepy town. There were some exceptions: A few old men armed themselves with rusty guns and swords, pitchforks, shovels, and pick-axes and assembled in the evenings to guard the town against a possible enemy attack. Their maneuvers consisted of commands given and not heeded. Most onlookers laughed at the spectacle.

59

Tillie Pierce at the time of the battle of Gettysburg
(courtesy of the Adams County Historical Society)

But the black families who resided in the southwestern part of Gettysburg took the threat of a rebel invasion seriously. Afraid of capture and a return to slavery, they packed up and left town. Fifteen-year-old Tillie Pierce watched their exodus:

> *I can see them yet; men and women with bundles as large as old-fashioned feather ticks slung across their backs, almost bearing them to the ground. Children also, carrying their bundles, and striving in vain to keep up. They hurried along; crowding and running against each other in their confusion; children stumbling, falling and crying. Mothers anxious for their offspring would stop for a moment to hurry them up, saying, "Fo de Lod's sake, you chillen, cum right long quick! If dem rebs dun kotch you, dey tear you all up."*

Ten-year-old Charles McCurdy observed how the cashier of the local bank locked up his counter, packed his cash into a valise, and joined the departing throng. "To be in the fashion," the boy later wrote, "I kept my most cherished possessions in a little box, ready for shipment, feeling quite important at the thought of danger. But I suspect that even the most hardened looter would not have found there anything to interest him."

Thirteen-year-old William Bayley, who lived on a farm three miles northwest of town cared more about horses than anything else he owned. On an evening in mid-June he joined his father and a group of neighbors and headed for Harrisburg, the capital city. "After having worked on the farm all day," he remembered, "I rode one horse and led another through the night." They stayed with a farmer friend, helped him harvest his wheat crop, and then returned home without encountering any enemies.

But come they did! On June 26, tired from a morning of haying, William was awakened from his after-lunch nap by the shouts of his neighbors: "The Rebs are coming." The boy ran to the barn, barefooted and coatless, to help his father saddle two of their best horses. He mounted "Nellie," a beautiful chestnut mare, and he and his father were off to the north. They rode all day and into the night and put up with a farmer who gave them food and shelter. The next morning, they were surprised by the sudden appearance of four Confederate cavalrymen. "While some of the men [on the farm] got into a heated argument with the soldiers over the war," William Bayley remembered, "my father . . . and I worked our way to the barn . . . contrived to get our horses . . . and rode back the thirty odd miles to our home."

Tillie Pierce encountered the first contingent of Confederate soldiers on her way home from school:

> What a horrible sight! There they were, human beings! clad almost in rags, covered with dust, riding wildly pell-mell down the hill toward our home! shouting, yelling most unearthly, cursing, brandishing their revolvers, and firing right and left. . . . They wanted horses, clothing, anything and almost everything they could conveniently carry away.

Tillie was much distressed when the Confederates took her favorite horse. "I was very much attached to the animal for she was gentle and very pretty," she wrote. "We frequently saw the Rebels riding [her] up and down the street, until at last she became so lame she could hardly get along. That was the last we saw of her, and I felt that I had been robbed of a dear friend."

Charles McCurdy had a more pleasant encounter with the invading rebels. Across the street from his home was a cake and candy shop that had been secured by the owner with wooden shutters and iron bars. When the Confederates learned that behind the bars was a stock of molasses taffy and gingercakes they had him open his store. "Hilarious boys in gray were giving him a new idea of trading," remembered little Charlie. "He was doing the business of his life, handing out candy in exchange for Confederate money. One big trooper came out of the shop with his hat full of candy and . . . gave me a handful."

In a few days the rebels moved on toward the north and west. Around noon on June 30, Union cavalry began to arrive from the south. The citizens of Gettysburg greeted them with joy and a great feeling of relief. "We were all down at Huber's corner looking at some of our men who were passing through town on their way . . . to attack the rebels," wrote seventeen-year-old Jennie McCreary in a letter to her sister on July 22, 1863.

Tillie Pierce remembered:

> It was to me a novel and grand sight. . . . for then I knew we had protection, and I felt they were our dearest friends. . . . A crowd of "us girls" were standing on the corner of Washington and High Streets as the soldiers passed by. Desiring to encourage them . . . my sister started the old war song "Our Union Forever." As some of us did not know the whole of the piece we kept repeating the chorus.

Little Charlie McCurdy sat on the top rail of a fence and watched the Union cavalry ride by. He offered them cherries from a branch "filled with the beautiful red fruit which was more alluring to the eye than to the palate" and then joined the company of small boys who tagged along at the tail end of the procession to watch the soldiers make camp, put up their tents, and prepare for supper. That night Union troops camped on the ridges west and north, between the town and the enemy.

Tillie Pierce and her sister stayed up late, preparing bouquets of flowers, intending to show the soldiers the next morning how welcome they would be. "As we lay down for the night," she wrote later, "little did we think what the morrow would bring forth."

The First Day of the Battle: July 1, 1863

At dawn on July 1, a Confederate infantry officer under General Richard Ewell's command led his men to Gettysburg to commandeer a supply of shoes for his footsore men. On their march from Carlisle, the Confederates had captured a battalion of school cadets. Fifteen-year-old John C. Early, nephew of Confederate General Richard Early, was traveling as a courier with Ewell's troops and observed what happened to the cadets. "They had marched out gallantly to the defense of their country," the boy from Virginia remembered, "but were not taken seriously by the Confederate officers, who simply transferred their army shoes and stockings to their own needy soldiers and left the lads to walk home bare-footed, in a less dignified style than they had started out."

About three miles north of Gettysburg, the Confederate advance guard ran into General John Buford's Union cavalry. Leander Warren, age fifteen, was in the Union camp that morning with his friends, helping out by riding cavalry horses to a creek for water. He left camp when the first shot was fired. "The bugles began to blow and the men got their horses ready," he remembered. "We thought we had better start for home. . . . When we got up to the ridge we stopped and looked back to see what was going on. . . . Some of the boys wanted to see where the shells were coming from, so they climbed up trees nearby. About that time a shell came over that way—they did not climb down, but fell down."

William Bayley had left his farm around nine o'clock that morning and was heading for Gettysburg. In company with several friends his age, he arrived on the top of Seminary Ridge, stopped for breath and surveyed the situation. No troops were in sight. The boys began to pick ripe raspberries. William remembered:

> *Two boys and myself went along the ridge and, in the absorbing interest of filling our stomachs with berries, forgot all about war and rumors of war for the time being until startled by the discharge of a cannon, the sharp impact of which made us jump. . . . This was instantly followed by a rapid succession of discharges and we three boys broke for the open. . . . One of my brothers, about nine years old, a cousin of my age and I . . . perched ourselves on the topmost rail of the road fence. . . . But our gallery seats . . . began to have features of discomfort when we noticed coming over the nearest hill, great masses of troops and clouds of dust; how the first wave swelled into successive waves, gray masses with the glint of steel . . . filling the highway, spreading out into the fields, and still coming on and on. . . . We waited not until we would see 'the whites of their eyes' but until they were but a few hundred yards between us and the [Federal] advance column, and then we departed for home . . . decorously and in order as became boys who had pre-empted seats to see a battle but found conditions too hot for comfort.*

That morning Charlie McCurdy, curious as ever, had wandered into Buford's camp and found it deserted. He turned back to town but was distracted by a small sword that had been driven into the ground. As he tugged away, a young Union officer rode by, and seeing the boy's fruitless efforts, got off his horse, pulled out the sword, and handed it to him with a smile. Then he mounted his horse and rode over the ridge into battle.

> *At this moment cannons began to boom and I had my first experience of war. A shell burst a few hundred yards in front. I ran for the road and when I reached it found my father hurrying toward me. . . . I clung to the sword but as the pace became faster it proved too much of a burden and as we passed a field of growing corn I threw it among the foliage. . . . By the time we reached home . . . there was heavy cannonading and the musket fire was continuous, making a rattling sound like heavy wagons being rapidly driven over a stony pike or like hail falling on a tin roof.*

Every Confederate and Union division in the area now converged on Gettysburg. Union officers rode through town, warning citizens to take to their cellars. Most residents obeyed; many shared their cellars with neighbors or relatives. Charlie McCurdy's mother hastily gathered a few things she thought might be needed and went to their grandmother's home. Grandmother was ninety years old. During the cannonading she was taken into the cellar, a strip of carpet laid on the floor, and there she sat in stately dignity in her rocking chair until the danger was past.

Not everyone took to cellar life with the same resilient spirit. Annie Young confessed in a letter to her cousin Mina that "all I could do was to sit in the cellar corner and cry. The firing of the musketry was more rapid than the ticking of a watch and for every gun fired there was a shriek." But seven-year-old Annie Skelly remembered a funny incident she witnessed when she was hiding out that day in her neighbor's cellar:

A German from the other end of town . . . came to the cellar for shelter. While there he was sitting on the end of a barrel when suddenly the top fell in under his weight, to the amusement of all there. We did not know whether a shell hit him or what. When we pulled him out by the head he said in broken English, "I believe I fell in the barrel" and then we all laughed.

Annie Young described the retreat of the Union forces in a letter written on July 5, 1863: "By noon our men were all around us, had their batteries, some of them, in our backyard . . . We sat in the cellar from then until near dark. Our men who were exhausted & wounded kept pouring into the cellar until it was so close & offensive from the blood and water on the muddy floor that we could hardly endure it."

Many teenagers tried to help the retreating Union soldiers as best they could. Wrote seventeen-year-old Jennie McCreary in a letter to her sister Julia on July 22, 1863:

I went over to Weaver's to help them roll bandages. We had not rolled many before we saw the street filled with wounded men. . . . Oh, it was sickening to see them and hear their groans. . . . I never thought I could do anything about a wounded man but I find I had a little more nerve than I thought I had. . . . The tears came only once and that was when the first soldier came in the house. He had walked from the field and was almost exhausted. He threw himself in the chair and said, "O girls, I have as good a home as you. If I were only there!" He fainted directly afterward. That was the only time I cried.

Fifteen-year-old Albertus McCreary ministered to the thirsty:

It was about noon . . . the street was full of Union soldiers, running and pushing each other, sweaty and black from powder and dust. They called to us for water. We got great buckets of water and tin dippers, and supplied them as fast as we could from the porch at the side of the house off the main street.... While we were carrying water to the soldiers, a small drummer boy ran up the porch, and handing me his drum, said, "Keep this for me." I took it, ran down the cellar steps and hid it under a pile of shavings. He looked to be about twelve years old.... We were so busy that we did not notice how close the fighting was until, about half a block away, we saw hand-to-hand conflicts.... We kept right on distributing water until an officer rode his horse up on the pavement ... and said, "All you good people go down in your cellars or you will all be killed."

Leander Warren's home was west of town along a wagon road. He, too, heard the retreating Union soldiers cry, "Water, water!" His mother placed a dishpan on the window while the boy and his sisters brought fresh water from the well. They dipped it out for the fleeing soldiers as they passed by. Union officers had to draw swords to force their men back to the ranks. "They fought so that we were just between the armies," the boy remembered, "with dead men and horses lying along the street. During this time we were in the cellar peeping out the cellar windows."

Even young Charlie McCurdy was not spared the sight of death: "Beside the little front porch that occupied half the sidewalk around our home, lay two dead Union soldiers," he wrote later. "I had never before seen a dead man, and yet I do not recall that I was shocked, so quickly does war brutalize. The wounded I had seen, the fierce excitement that ranged around me, had blunted even my young sensibilities."

By mid-afternoon, the Confederates had pushed the Union forces back through the town. Wrote Annie Young on July 5, 1863: "About 4 o'clock our house fell into Rebel hands: they charged right thro our hall. One fierce looking fellow came in the cellar with his gun pointed. I immediately screamed 'we'll surrender'. ... I thot I would surely die on the spot."

Albertus McCreary similarly remembered:

Suddenly the outer cellar doors were pulled open, and five Confederate soldiers jumped down among us. We thought our last day had come.... One fellow—I can see him yet—with a red face covered with freckles and very red hair, dirty and sweaty, with his gun in his hand, said, "We are looking for Union soldiers." "There are none here," Father answered. But the soldier said he would have to search, and that we could go upstairs, and the danger was over for a time.

Upstairs, the searchers found thirteen Union men hiding—some under the beds, one under the piano, and others in closets. The prisoners were brought into the dining room, where the officer-in-charge took down their names. The boy's father invited *both* Confederate and Union soldiers for dinner, and all were glad to accept the invitation. "Now that they had stopped fighting," noted the boy with astonishment, "both sides seemed to be on the best of terms, and laughed and chatted like old comrades."

Not everyone was intimidated by the appearance of the Confederate troops. Liberty Augusta Hollinger, who was sixteen at the time, remembered how the rebels took possession of her neighbor's home and ate all the biscuits they found in the cupboard. "Several called to Julia, my [fourteen-year-old] sister, who was on our balcony, and asked for butter for their biscuits. She saucily answered, 'If you are hungry you can eat them as they are.' They laughed and went back to the house."

By seven o'clock in the evening, much of Gettysburg was occupied by the Confederates, who brought their wounded from the battlefield to homes and yards throughout the city. Most soldiers were courteous and considerate to the town's inhabitants, who had emerged, dazed and frightened, from their cellars. Annie Young, who only hours earlier had thought she would die, found herself serving tea to General Ewell and his staff:

> *They were all very polite & kind, I sat at the head of the table & gave them their coffee so I had a fine opportunity to see them all. With a few I was completely captivated. We freely gave them our opinion on the war. They were not at all offended but said if our men had half the spirit they would fight better.*

Leander Warren overheard a conversation between his father and a Confederate officer who rode up to their house in the evening to check on his tired men resting on the pavement.

> *He said to my father, "Why is it you are not in the army?" Father said, "I am too old, but I have a son in my place." Then the officer asked, "What are your sentiments?" Father replied, "I am a Union man." The officer said, "You are the kind of man I like to talk to." They argued the question in good humor for quite a while.*

When Leander's father learned that the officer had not eaten all day, he offered him some freshly baked shortcake that was gladly accepted. So were the chicken soup, the bread, and the cherry pies that William Bayley's mother baked for her Confederate "guests" on their farm. The boy remembered:

> *With some of these "Johnny Rebs" I became quite chummy and discussed the situation [on the battlefield] with all the confidence and optimism of a [young] boy. . . . However, when they said they were going to lick the Yan-*

kees out of their boots, and I said "you can't do it," I had the best of the argument in the end.

The retreating Federal troops, meanwhile, had rallied and established defensive positions along Cemetery Ridge south of town. Hills overlooked the Union positions at both ends: Culp's and Cemetery Hills on the right, Little and Big Round Top on the left. In Gettysburg that night, Annie Young looked up to the sky: "The moon was shining brightly in the heavens, while on earth scattered everywhere were the dead and the wounded, moaning with pain. . . . I thought I had been transferred to some strange place, so different did it seem from the home I had seen in the morning."

It was near midnight when courier John Early finally tracked down the Confederate headquarters—the home of the superintendent of the Gettysburg poorhouse. It had been a busy day for the boy. Considered by his uncle too young to serve on the battlefield, he had been directed to "supervise" the stretcher men who carried the wounded into town.

The sights he saw that day would be etched in his memory forever. He saw a German Union soldier, lying on the ground with the top of his skull taken off, bleeding to death. Near him was a dead officer from New York whose pockets had been turned out. Lying close to him on the ground were two papers, one of them a furlough permit, issued two days earlier, to allow him to go and get married; the other was a letter from his bride-to-be, expressing her happiness about the approaching event.

Now the boy was looking for his father, Captain Samuel H. Early, and his uncle, the general. He found them in conversation with General Lee, who had arrived in Gettysburg in the middle of the afternoon. A fateful decision had been made that night: The Confederates would attempt to take the heights on which the Union forces were entrenched on the very next day. "At the end of the discussion," the boy remembered, "my father came up and I went away with him to spend the night in camp, but first we got sufficient corn to feed our horses."

The Second Day of the Battle: July 2, 1863

Through the night the two armies gathered reinforcements. The people of Gettysburg slept fitfully. William Bayley and his mother were alone in their farmhouse northwest of town. Some time after midnight they heard a knock at the kitchen door and went downstairs. William remembered:

At the door we found a little fellow in a gray uniform, hardly taller than I and only a couple of years older, who said he had been through the battle of the day before, that his company had been cut to pieces, that he was from

*North Carolina, was tired of fighting and never wanted to see another bat-
tle—would not mother conceal him somewhere until the battle was over. He
was given a suit of clothes and sent to the garret where the feather beds were
stored for the summer and several old bedsteads not in use, told to find a bed
and in the morning change his gray uniform for civilian attire.*

On July 2, some of the Confederate "visitors" from the day before were
back at the Bayley farm for a breakfast of bread and "black spread," as
they called the apple butter. Little did they know that the silent boy who
broke off cherry branches for them as they passed beneath the orchard
trees was one of their former comrades-in-arms. They were jubilant
about the results of the first day's battle. "We had to hear 'I told you so!
Didn't I tell you that we would whip the Yanks?' sung to us . . . all . . .
day," William Bayley recalled.

Jennie McCreary was back home with her family in Gettysburg. "We
heard nothing but a continual roar of cannon and musketry," she wrote to
her sister Julia three weeks later. "The firing began at about four in the
morning and lasted till dark. . . . We didn't mind the shells so much. . . . We
were getting used to them; the greatest danger was from the sharpshooters."

Tillie Pierce found herself in a much more dangerous spot. The day before, she had gone along with a neighbor to the supposed safety of Jacob
Weikert's farmhouse, three miles south of Gettysburg. It was located on
the eastern slope of the Round Tops, near the southern end of the Union
line where the fiercest fighting of the day would take place. Wrote she:

*My attention was called to numerous rough boxes which had been placed
along the road just outside the garden fence. Ominous . . . as was the sight
presented, it nevertheless did not prevent some of the soldiers from joking.
One of the men nearby, addressed with the remark that there was no telling
how soon he would be out in one of them, replied: "I will consider myself
very lucky if I get one."*

Around noon she spotted dead soldiers lying on the ground behind
the house. They had been picked off by rebel sharpshooters. In the afternoon heavy cannonading began on Little and Big Round Top, just back of
the farm. "It began very unexpectedly," she remembered. "We were all
terror-stricken and hardly knew what to do."

Two teenaged boys were among the Union troops who saw the fiercest
fighting that afternoon and left eyewitness accounts. One was the drummer boy William Bardeen from the First Massachusetts Regiment. At two
o'clock in the afternoon he sat in the limbs of a tree watching the Confederate wagon trains and artillery moving toward the Round Tops and the
Union's left flank. His diary entry for July 2, 1863, reads:

Nothing of importance occurred until afternoon when the attack was sud-denly made upon our left and the fight commenced in earnest. Our men were driven [back] at first, but the 5th Corps came up and formed on our left which ended any doubts as to the result.

Private Theodore Gerrish of the Twentieth Maine Regiment fought un-der the command of Colonel Joshua Chamberlain on Little Round Top. Orders were to hold it "at all hazards." If this little mountain was to fall into Confederate hands, they would be able to blow the Union lines apart with their artillery. Theodore Gerrish wrote later:

Imagine if you can, nine small companies of infantry . . . three hundred men . . . on the extreme flank of an army of 80,000, put there to hold the key of the entire position against a force at least ten times their number. . . . The conflict opens. The carnage begins . . . a terrible medley of cries, shouts, cheers, groans, prayers, curses, bursting shells, whizzing rifle bullets and clanging steel. . . . Our line is pressed back so far that our dead are within the lines of the enemy. Our ammunition is nearly all gone. . . . We must ad-vance or retreat. The order is given, "Fix bayonets!" and the steel shanks of the bayonets rattle upon the rifle barrels. "Charge bayonets! Charge!"

The attacking Confederates were taken by surprise, wavered, broke lines, and fled for their lives. Little Round Top held. The battle went on until dark. Just before nightfall, William Bayley went to the portico roof above the main porch of his farmhouse to watch the show. He was more than five miles north of the worst fighting, but he could hear the cease-less thundering of artillery and the screams peculiar to shots and shells when hurtling through the air. He saw the flashes of fire from bursting shells as darkness came on.

Tillie Pierce, at the southern end of the battle line, witnessed the hu-man cost of the violent encounter. She wrote later:

On this evening, the number of wounded brought to [Weikert's farm] was indeed appalling. They were laid in different parts of the house. The orchard and space around the buildings were covered with the shattered and dying and the barn became more and more crowded. The scene had become terrible beyond description.

Back in Gettysburg, Leander Warren's family was urged by the Con-federate officer they had fed the night before to leave town and go north, to the rear of the army. The boy remembered him saying, "I know you will loose whatever you have, but take your horse and wagon and take all your best things, I will send an escort along to see you safely through our lines." One of his men, with a brass horn around his neck, conducted

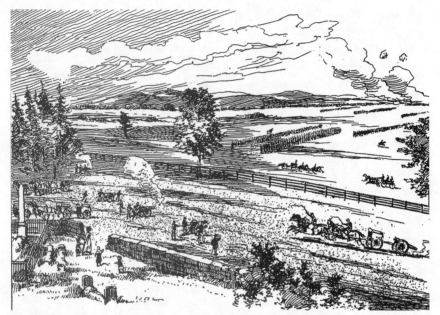

Fleeing from Danger (At Gettysburg, New York: W. L. Borland, 1889)

Leander and his parents through the Confederate lines. The boy saw dead men lying along both sides of the road—their bodies had turned black in the hot July sun.

Charlie McCurdy and his family stayed in town. "Cannons thundered and musketry fire rattled all day," the boy remembered. "Much of the time we spent in the cellar. We had no bread, but ham, apple butter and preserves and fared well compared with the poor fellows who were being killed and mangled all about us."

Yet in the midst of the slaughter and suffering, there were fleeting moments when civility returned to the town of Gettysburg. Liberty Augusta Hollinger remembered that in the evening of July 2 a number of Confederates came into her family's yard and asked for some supper. The Hollingers had no food to give.

> *They then politely asked us girls to sing for them. [My sister] Julia . . . told them that we would not sing to please Confederates, but that possibly our boys in blue might hear us and be cheered. So we sang a number of our own Union songs with which we were familiar. Each time the Confederates would respond with one of their southern songs. Presently an officer rode into the yard and said to one of the men, "Cap, you'd better be careful about these songs." The captain answered, "Why that's all right. They sing their battle songs and then we sing ours."*

As the sun set, the Union's left and right still held.

Early in the night a Confederate officer and a couple of his lieutenants stopped by the Bayley farm northwest of town, asked for accommodations and were shown to the spare room, containing two beds, where they spent the night. Passing the door of the room where the officers were quartered, William Bayley noticed a sword in its scabbard, a belt, and pistol holders standing outside of the door, which was shut. "I marvelled that a man should be so careless when in the house of an enemy, " mused the boy. When he awoke early next morning, the men had gone back to the battlefield.

The Third Day of the Battle: July 3, 1863

In her July letter to her sister Julia, Jennie McCreary expressed the sentiment of civilians and soldiers alike:

> *All felt that this day must decide who should conquer. . . . It was comparatively quiet until . . . the afternoon, and then the cannonading began . . . such cannonading no one ever heard. Nothing can be compared to it, one who has never heard it cannot form any idea how terrible it is.*

Tillie Pierce at the Weikert farm south of town was trying to return to Gettysburg. She and her companions had been warned by the Union soldiers who had planted cannons on two sides of the house that there would likely be hard fighting around the farm.

> *When we reached the carriages, and were about to get in, a shell came screaming through the air directly overhead. I was so frightened that I gave a shriek and sprang into the barn [where the wounded were]. Even with their suffering, the poor fellows could not help laughing at my terror. . . . One of them near me said: "My child, if that had hit you, you would not have had time to jump."*

The massive artillery barrage by the Confederates began around one o'clock in the afternoon and was intended to soften up the Union soldiers before an attack on their center. Union shells, in turn, took a toll on the Confederate infantry waiting in the woods. After about an hour, the Federal guns fell silent, to conserve ammunition and to lure the rebels out into the open fields.

Corporal Thomas Galwey from Cleveland, Ohio, was among an infantry detachment that had been positioned at the most advanced skirmish line. Suddenly, a rebel sharpshooter who had been in a tree nearby began shouting, "Don't fire Yanks!" Wrote Galwey in his diary:

A man with his gun slung over the shoulder came out from the tree. . . . The man had a canteen in his hand, and when he had come half-way to us, we saw him (God bless him) kneel down and give a drink to one of our wounded who lay there beyond us. Of course we cheered the Reb, and some-one shouted, "Bully for you! Johnny!"

It was a little after three o'clock in the afternoon when Confederate Major General George Pickett, gave the order to charge: "Up men and to your posts! Don't forget today that you are from old Virginia." Three divisions of rebel soldiers started out of the woods at a brisk, steady pace. Thomas Galwey watched them come:

We saw the enemy with colors flying advancing in columns in mass. . . . I had often read of battles and of charges, had been in not a few myself; but until this moment I had not gazed upon so grand a sight as was presented by that beautiful mass of grey . . . as it came on . . . cheering their peculiar cheer, right towards the crest of the hills which we and our batteries were to defend.

Union artillery on Cemetery Ridge and Little Round Top now opened fire on the advancing lines. On and on the Confederates came, still brave and cheering. They breached the stone wall where the Union batteries were standing. "Then, in the nick of time," Galwey wrote, "a portion of the 29th New York charges them. . . . The enemy, now broken and disorganized and far from any support, begins to retire. The retreat is turned into a flight."

By the end of the day, half of the rebel forces who had marched out of the woods had been killed, wounded, or captured. Observed the young corporal from Ohio, "Towards dark all became quiet. Both armies were now exhausted. . . . Men ran about everywhere seeking wounded comrades, not forgetting . . . to do many kindnesses to the enemy's wounded who everywhere lay mixed with ours."

Tillie Pierce, still at Weikert's farm, saw nothing but desolation:

I fairly shrank back at the awful sight presented. The approaches were crowded with wounded, dying and dead. . . . By this time amputating benches had been placed about the house. . . . I saw them lifting the poor men upon it . . . I saw the surgeons hastily put a cattle horn over the mouths of the wounded ones . . . and learned that was their mode of administering chloroform, in order to produce unconsciousness. But the effect, in some instances, was not produced; for I saw the wounded throwing themselves wildly about, and shrieking with pain while the operation was going on. . . . Just outside the yard I noticed a pile of limbs higher than the fence. It was a ghastly sight."

Only gradually did the residents of Gettysburg realize that the battle had ended. "During the night we knew we were victorious," wrote Jennie McCreary. "We saw the rebel wagon trains moving off." With them was the young nephew of General Early, whose father had been wounded in the leg during the third day of the battle. His uncle had ordered him to take care of his dad. The boy found a corn buggy, hitched his father's riding horse to it, and joined Lee's retreating wagon trains. They were heading home for Virginia.

After the Battle

On the morning of July 4, 1863, the citizens of Gettysburg heard a noisy demonstration. Union men had arrived in the public square. The townsfolk came out of their homes and cellars to greet them, knowing now that they were safe.

Jennie McCreary wrote to her sister, "How happy every one felt! None but smiling faces were to be seen. It was indeed a joyful Fourth for us." Tillie Pierce was still on Weikert's farm when she heard the cheering:

> *On the summits, in the valleys, everywhere we heard the soldiers hurrahing for the victory that had been won. The troops on our right, at Culp's Hill, caught up the joyous sound as it came rolling on from the Round Tops on our left, and soon the whole line of Blue rejoiced. . . . We were all glad that the storm had passed. . . . But oh! the horror and desolation that remained.*

Drummer boy William Bardeen and Corporal Thomas Galwey spent July 4 and 5 burying the dead. Wrote the drummer boy in his diary: "Went out on the battlefield. An awful sight, men, horses, all lying in heaps as far as the eye can reach."

Thomas Galwey noted in his journal: "We have been picking up such of our dead as we could recognize. Each regiment selects a suitable place and puts a headboard on each individual grave. The unrecognized dead are left to the last to be buried in long trenches."

The twenty-four hundred inhabitants of Gettysburg were left with ten times as many wounded to tend to. All public buildings and barns for miles around were filled with injured men.

Charlie McCurdy described a makeshift hospital in his family's barn: "The men lay on the threshing floor, each on a single blanket, without any covering of any kind. . . . They were a pitiful sight."

The McCurdys, like other townfolk, nursed wounded soldiers in their home. Most of those taken into private homes were Union men, but Charlie's parents took care of an elderly Confederate general "who was

William Black, age twelve, wounded by an exploding shell (courtesy of the Library of Congress)

delightful and appreciative . . . [and] fond of children." Charlie's little sisters were frequent visitors to his room. But the boy was more intrigued by the general's aide, who had been a sailor: "One day in the privacy of the stable he took off his shirt and showed me his back on which a full rigged ship was tattooed, a very unusual and thrilling exhibit."

Ten-year-old Charlie McCurdy and fifteen-year-old Albertus Mc-Creary combed the battlefield for relics, which were in great demand by the visitors who came to Gettysburg in the weeks to come. Among Charlie's prized possessions was a store of bullets that had hit a boulder or tree, giving them a grotesque shape. Albertus and his friends sometimes found pockets of bullets in a pile—weighing eight to ten pounds. Lead was scarce at this time, and the boys went "into business," making thirteen cents a pound. Sometimes they became careless. Remembered Albertus:

A schoolmate of mine . . . had been hunting bullets on Cemetery Hill. He found a shell, and, the contents not coming out fast enough for him, he struck it upon a rock on which he was sitting, and made a spark which exploded the shell. We carried him home, and the surgeons did what they could for him, but he never regained consciousness and died in about an hour.

Cemetery records show that two boys were killed that way: James Culp, age sixteen, on September 9, and Allen Frazer, age thirteen, on November 20, 1863. The day before, on November 19, President Lincoln had come to Gettysburg to dedicate the National Soldiers' Cemetery.

Annie Skelly, age seven, watched the parade in front of the courthouse. A man lifted the little girl up so she could see Lincoln. "The street was crowded with people," she wrote later, "leaving only enough room for him to pass on his horse. He would turn from side to side, looking at the people on either side when he passed with a solemn face. He looked rather odd on such a small horse." Charlie McCurdy watched the procession as it moved to the cemetery. The boy was impressed by the president's great height, "which was emphasized by his high silk hat and his long frock coat."

Albertus McCreary sat only a few feet away from the platform where Mr. Lincoln delivered his Gettysburg Address. Later he shook hands with the president. He would never forget Lincoln's good strong grasp. The most vivid impression left on Liberty Ann Hollinger was the "inexpressible sadness on his face." The battle was over, but the war would go on.

— 6 —

I's so 'Fraid
God's Killed, Too!

O N THE EVENING OF JULY 3, 1863, when the battle in faraway Gettysburg had turned to a victory for the Union, James Newton, a teenage soldier from Wisconsin, wrote to his parents from his campsite near Vicksburg, Mississippi: "It is nearly night . . . but I guess I will have time to tell you the good news: Vicksburg is ours at last. *The 4th of July scared them so that they concluded it was best to give up,* and for my part I think it is the best thing they could have done."

For more than six weeks, thirty-one thousand Confederate soldiers and four thousand townspeople, including more than a thousand children, had been surrounded by Union forces, isolated from friends and outside relief. More than two hundred Union guns had pounded Vicksburg every day from land, while Federal gunboats battered it from the Mississippi River. The town, stretching for nearly a mile along the river, its streets rising up the hills from the waterfront, had been mauled as no community had ever been in the history of the American people. In the beleaguered city, women and children, black and white, had carried on their daily lives with good humor and an indomitable spirit. They had passed their trial by fire.

The first heavy shelling had begun in the evening on April 16, 1863, when Admiral David Porter's gunboats, under cover of dark, headed down the hairpin bend of the river that led past Vicksburg's bluffs. A few minutes later all hell broke loose. General Ulysses S. Grant was present to see the show with his wife and two young sons, twelve-year old Frederick and ten-year-old Ulysses Jr. They were gathered on the upper deck of the transport ship *Magnolia*, anchored in the middle of the river, just beyond the range of the heaviest guns.

Twelve-year-old Fred Grant later recalled: "On board our boat, my father and I stood side by side on the hurricane deck. He was quietly smoking, but an intense light shone in his eyes." "Magnificent but terrible," Grant called the sight. But the noise of the bursting shells terrified ten-year-old Ulysses Jr. Wrote the general's aide, James Harriet Wilson: "He sat on my knees with his arms around my neck, and as each crash came, he nervously clasped me closer, and finally became so frightened that he was put to bed."

The people of Vicksburg, both soldiers and civilians, swarmed into the streets. Among the women were officers' wives in their most fashionable attire who had been attending a spring ball sponsored by the commander of the Confederate garrison. Mary Loughborough, mother of a two-year-old daughter, had come over from Jackson, Mississippi, to visit with her husband, who was stationed in Vicksburg. When the shelling started, she remembered, "there was nothing but confusion and alarm."

The shelling lasted until midnight. The Confederates sank one transport ship, but the first wave of the Union fleet had passed, and the second would follow in a week. On April 30, Grant's forces crossed the river, without opposition, at Bruinsburg. Like a scythe, Grant's army now hooked into central Mississippi, then cut back westward toward Vicksburg. The noose was slowly tightening.

Dora Miller, a young bride from New Orleans and a Union sympathizer, wrote in her diary on May 1:

> It is settled at last that we shall spend the time of siege in Vicksburg. . . . Sitting at work as usual, listening to the distant sound of bursting shells, apparently aimed at the courthouse, there came a nearer explosion; the house shook and a tearing sound was followed by terrific screams from the kitchen. I rushed thither, but met in the hall the cook's little girl America, bleeding from a wound in the forehead, and fairly dancing with fright and pain, while she uttered fearful yells. . . . Her mother bounded in, her black face ashy from terror. "Oh! Miss V., my child is killed and the kitchen tore up." Seeing America was too lively to be killed, I consoled Martha and hastened to the kitchen. Evidently a shell had exploded just outside, sending three or four pieces through. When order was restored I endeavored to impress on Martha's mind the necessity for calmness. . . . Looking round . . . there stood a group of Confederate soldiers chiming in, "Yes, it's no use hollerin."

So they settled in for the siege, calmly, without hollering!

All the people of Vicksburg could do now was wait and hope that Grant's army would be annihilated on their way to Jackson. But they hoped in vain: On May 14, Grant captured the capital of Jefferson Davis's home state, the third capital the South had lost. Twelve-year-old Fred

Grant rode off on his own to the state house, ahead of the main body of the Federal troops, He wrote later:

> *When I arrived at the capitol, the Confederate troops were passing. They were in haste and paid no heed to my presence, although I wore a blue uniform. I was very small, very wet, much splashed with mud, and altogether unattractive. I was the only "Yankee" around.*

But soon the boy was joined by a Union cavalryman who stopped at the capitol, dismounted and entered. Minutes later, Fred looked up from the streets and saw the officer high in the domed cupola of the building, raising the Union flag over the fallen city. Fred remounted his pony and rode off to meet his father. Together they went to Bowen House, Jackson's finest hotel. General Grant was given the rooms that had been occupied by the Confederate General Joseph Johnston on the previous night. Father and son had plenty of reasons to celebrate.

Meanwhile, Mary Loughborough and her young daughter had returned to Jackson from her visit to her husband—only to find Union troops entering her hometown. Back she went to Vicksburg—and there she stayed with her little girl throughout the siege. To a friend's question of how she managed to live there, she replied: "After one is accustomed to the change, we do not mind it; but *becoming* accustomed, that was the trial."

The people of Vicksburg dug some five hundred caves in the yellow clay hillsides, some with several rooms fitted out with rugs, beds, and rocking chairs and staffed with black servants. Others laid their beds in their cellars and brought in what food they could find. In the flickering light of a homemade candle Dora Miller mused over "accumulated bottles [which] told of the banquet hall deserted" and consoled herself with the thought: "A city besieged is a city taken—so if we live through it we shall be out of the Confederacy." "It was living like plant roots," a woman wrote in her diary. The Union troops began calling Vicksburg "prairie dog village."

Slowly Grant's troops felt their way to the high ground surrounding the city. On Sunday, May 17, Mary Loughborough was on her way to church when she saw the retreating columns of Confederate soldiers who had been repulsed by Federal troops at the Big Black River. They were limping through town, unarmed but followed by ambulances, gun carriages, and wagons in aimless confusion. "I feared leaving my little one for any length of time," she wrote, "if there were any prospects of an engagement." But at twilight, her spirits lifted as she saw fresh troops from Warrenton marching by, headed for the entrenchments in the rear of the city where her husband was posted. Dora Miller observed, "Two or three bands on the courthouse hill . . . began playing 'Dixie' and 'Bonnie Blue

Flag,' and drums began to beat all about; I suppose they were rallying the scattered army."

During the battle at the Big Black River, Young Fred Grant had been watching some retreating Confederates when a sharpshooter on the opposite bank fired at him, hitting the boy in the leg. He remembered:

> *The wound, though slight, was very painful, and I must have become extremely pale, for just at this time [a Union] colonel came dashing up and asked me what had happened to me. I answered that I had been killed, a piece of news no doubt surprising to him. He asked me where I was hit. I replied, "in the left leg." He told me to try and move my foot about which I found I could do very well. He then said, "All right, you are not dead; now let us get away from here quickly."*

On May 19, Grant's men attempted their first direct assault on Vicksburg. Mary Loughborough described her feelings during the bombardment:

> *We were terrified and much excited by the loud rush and scream of mortar shells; we ran to the small cave near the house. . . . The room I had so lately slept in had been struck by a fragment of a shell . . . and a large hole made in the ceiling. . . . Terror stricken, we remained crouched in the cave, while shell after shell followed each in quick succession. . . . [I was] cowering in a corner, holding my child to my heart. . . . As the day wore on, and we were still preserved, though the shells came as ever, we were somewhat encouraged.*

The numbing shock of terror had begun to wear off, and when the Union assault was beaten back, the spirit of the people of Vicksburg began to rise. For the first time, Grant had been halted—not beaten, just stopped, but this small success gave them a measure of hope. Then, three days later, came Grant's second assault. Lida Lord, the young daughter of a Episcopalian minister, remembered how the new troubles began. "Before sunset," she wrote, "a bombshell burst into the very center of the dining room [in the rectory of Christ Church], blowing out the roof and one side, crushing the well-spread table like an eggshell, and making a great yawning hole in the floor, into which disappeared supper, china, furniture . . . and our stock of butter and eggs."

The entire household—five children, their parents, and the servants—moved to the basement of Christ Church. Lida's little brother, William Lord Jr., remembered that night: His father, in clerical coat, a red smoking-cap on his head, was seated on an empty cask "looking like a pirate"; William's mother and sisters huddled around him on a coal heap; the servants in a neighboring coal-bin were moaning and praying; and the whole scene was lighted by the fitful glow of two tallow candles. As the shells shook the ground, four-year-old Lida began to cry. Her mother, trying to comfort her, said: "Don't cry, my darling, God will protect us." "But mamma," sobbed Lida, "I's so 'fraid God's killed too!"

On the Union side, young Fred Grant watched the fierce artillery assault by the Federal troops. Suddenly a small boy, no larger than himself, came running from the front, the blood streaming from a wound in his left side, crying: "General, our regiment is out of ammunition." Noted Fred:

> The little fellow, becoming weak from the loss of blood, looked up and said, "Caliber 68," and as he tottered, he was seized by two soldiers and carried to the rear. I went up to my father . . . and found to my surprise that his eyes were suffused with tears of sympathy for the brave boy.

For a second time, the Union troops were beaten back. Elisha Stockwell from Wisconsin wrote in his diary:

> The regiment charged the Reb's fortifications, but we were badly repulsed, loosing nearly one half of our number in killed and wounded in about ten minutes. After this we dug up to them. It was [only] two rods from the outside of our fort to the outside of the reb's fort. Moonlight nights they used to agree to have a talk, and both sides would get up on the breastworks and . . . laugh and sing songs for an hour at a time, then get down and commence shooting again.

The Union army settled in its lines, pounding the city day and night, while gunboats fired their naval guns and mortars from the river. The siege of Vicksburg would last forty-seven days.

Wrote James K. Newton to his parents in Wisconsin on May 24: "There is not much news, only that we have the rebels in a pretty tight place. They are completely surrounded and if we can't make them surrender any other way we can starve them out."

Throughout the Confederacy, horror stories began to proliferate about the effects of the siege and bombardments on the residents of Vicksburg. In faraway Richmond, Mary Chesnut heard about a three-year-old girl whose arm was shattered by a shell when she and her grandmother were about to leave the cave they had sought refuge in. "There was this poor little girl with her touchingly lovely face—and her arm gone," she wrote in her diary.

Despite such lurid accounts, the danger to the people of Vicksburg was more apparent than real. Fewer than a dozen civilians were killed as the siege progressed; three dozen were injured. Still, thousands of women and children had to endure the torment of living day and night under the threat of intense bombardment. Mary Loughborough wrote: "So constantly dropped the shells around the city, that the inhabitants all made preparations to live under the ground during the siege. . . . My husband had a cave made in a hill nearby. . . . Our new habitation was an excavation made in the earth, branching six feet from the entrance, forming a cave in the shape of a T. In one of the wings my bed fitted; the other I used as kind of a dressing room. . . . I could stand erect there."

Mrs. Loughborough and her daughter had the luxury of some privacy, but Reverend W. W. Lord, his wife, and their five children had to share their place of underground refuge with eight other families, their servants, and "other single persons." His daughter Lida Lord, dreaded the nights and the snakes in the cave. She remembered one night especially, when she shared her hiding place with sixty-five other persons, "packed in, black and white, like sardines in a box." She could not sleep much as there was constant moaning and crying. Several wounded soldiers lay on the cave floor, a big box filled with blankets held several babies, and a woman went into labor before her very eyes. She was grateful when "the blessed daylight came like heaven."

Lida's mother wrote, "The children bear themselves like little heroes. At night when the balls begin to fly like pigeons . . . and I call them to run to the cave, they spring up . . . like soldiers, slip on their shoes without a word and run up the hill to the cave." One of the youngsters who shared the Lords' cave was little Lucy McRae, buried alive when an exploding Federal shell collapsed part of their underground refuge. Mrs. Lord watched in horror: "A large piece of earth fell upon Mrs. McRae's little daughter . . . but for Mr. Lord's presence of mind she would have been killed or seriously injured."

Lucy later wrote about the incident that nearly took her life:

Everyone in the cave seemed to be dreadfully alarmed and excited when suddenly a shell came down on top of the hill, buried itself about six feet in the earth, and exploded. This caused a large mass of earth to slide . . . catching me under it. Dr. Lord, whose leg was caught and held by it, gave the alarm that a child was buried. Mother reached me first, and . . . with the assistance of Dr. Lord who was in agony . . . succeeded in getting my head out first. . . . They pulled me from under the mass of earth. The blood was gushing from my nose, eyes, ears, and mouth . . . but there were no bones broken. . . . During all this excitement there was a little baby boy born in the room dug out at the back of the cave. . . . The firing continued through the night and early next morning. . . . Mother decided to leave the cave . . . determined to risk her life at home with father. We left the cave about eight o'clock. . . . I was bent over from my injuries and could not run fast, though between the shells we would make the fastest time possible; watch-

Lucy McRae (courtesy Gordon Cotton, Vicksburg and Warren County Historical Society)

ing the shells, we learned to run toward them, to let them go over us if they would.

Lucy's father was horrified when he saw his bleeding daughter, and he immediately searched for another hiding place for his family. Close to their home, he found a small hill in which someone had dug a cave deep into the ground, too deep for a shell to pass through. Lucy's mother pitched a tent near the steps that led down to the cave, so that they could watch the shells as they came over the town. "They were beautiful at night," Lucy remembered.

Several days after her brush with death, Lucy was in the tent when a mortar shell rattled over her head. She barely had time to jump into a small hole the children had dug out in the side of the hill when a piece of shell came down into the tent, demolishing the washstand by which she had stood only moments earlier. "I sat, stunned with fear," the little girl remembered. "The shots fell thick and fast . . . the booming cannons sounded terrible. . . . When we finally could look out upon the daylight, it was with thankful hearts that we had been spared."

In the Union lines, James Newton took time out to write his mother:

I can distinctly hear the shells crash through the houses. Indeed some of the boys went so far as to say they could hear the screams of women and children, but—their ears must have been better than mine. . . . On the whole I guess they had their hands full. I can't pity the rebels themselves but it does seem too bad for the women and children in the city.

In the same letter, the young infantryman from Wisconsin described an encounter he had with the defenders of Vicksburg during a cessation of hostilities that allowed each party to bury their dead:

The "Rebs" were quite friendly to us while the white flag was up. They came out of their entrenchments and we went out of ours and met them down in the ravine which separates their breastwork from ours. We had a long talk. . . . They agreed with us perfectly on one thing: If the settlement of this war was left to the Enlisted men of both sides we would soon go home.

But the siege went on. Wrote Emma Balfour, the wife of a local physician, on May 27: "Nothing from the outside world yet. All day and all night the shells from the mortars are falling around us. . . . Most people spend their time entirely in the caves for there is no safety anywhere else. Indeed, there is no safety there. Several accidents have occurred. In one cave nearly a whole family were killed or crippled."

And on May 28, Dora Miller jotted in her diary: "We are utterly cut off from the world, surrounded by a circle of fire. . . . People do nothing but eat what they can get, sleep when they can, and dodge the shells. . . . The confinement is dreadful. . . . I do not know what others do but we read [Charles Dickens's novels] when I am not scribbling like this."

But the children were growing accustomed to the sounds of guns and learned to entertain themselves as best they could. Reverend W. W. Lord's family had moved into a private cave of their own, next to the camp of the officers of a Missouri brigade who in the opinion of young William Lord were "very merry gentlemen." The officers spent most of their evenings with the children, making the gloomy recesses of their cave echo with songs and laughter. By candlelight, they drew silhouettes of the children's faces in the soft clay walls and carved shelves for them on which to place candles, flowers, and books. They taught William and Lida Lord a gleeful parody of the song "Then Let the Old Folks Scold if They Will":

Then let the big guns boom if they will,
We'll be gay and happy still,
Gay and happy, gay and happy,
We'll be gay and happy still.

The children loved that song and, of course, the other favorites, "Dixie," "The Bonnie Blue Flag," and "Maryland, My Maryland." The whole family sang them with patriotic zest, "except my father," wrote William W. Lord Jr., "who could not sing a note." One of the soldiers even carved a set of Lilliputian knives and forks from a minie ball for the girls to play with, to their infinite pride and delight.

Throughout the entire siege the Lord children took comfort from their father, who opened Christ Church every day, rang the bell, and conducted services for the powder-grimed soldiers and shell-shocked civilians.

On May 30, Emma Balfour, the physician's wife, wrote in her diary:

The general impression is that they fire at the city . . . thinking that they will wear out the women and children and sick, and General John C. Pemberton will be obliged to surrender the place on that account; but they little know the spirit of the Vicksburg women and children if they expect this. Rather than let them know they are causing us any suffering I would be content to suffer martyrdom.

As May drew to a close, a spirit of timelessness crept into the city. Hours and days were no longer measured by the clocks or calendars but by the intervals when the shelling stopped—usually about eight in the morning, the same in the evening, and at noon. At the caves, meals were prepared when the shelling abated. The cooking had to be done outside, and the risk was too great to cook in the open with shells landing close by. Occasionally, erratic firing meant that people went without food for long periods of time. Young Lida Lord remembered that her family once had nothing to eat for twenty-four hours; finally when they did get a meal it was because one of their servants walked through the explosions to bring in a "tray of ham and butter." People tried to meet this exigency by baking large quantities of bread and subsisting on it and milk, providing their cows had not been killed. This was cold, dreary eating, meal after meal. "I eat with tears in my eyes," wrote Dora Miller.

Sleeping also depended upon the extent of the shelling rather than upon the coming of the night. Some children learned to sleep even in the heaviest bombardment, but most weary mothers did not, and a night during which there were few mortar explosions was regarded as a luxury. Occasions for washing and bathing were also dictated by the shelling, not by the amount of accumulated dirt or passage of time. Lida

Caves in Vicksburg (courtesy of the Chicago Historical Society)

Lord's mother wrote on June 1: "I have not been undressed now for nearly two weeks."

James Newton, the teenager from Wisconsin, watched from the Union lines. He wrote to his father in the first week of June:

> *It is a pretty sight to see the shells from the mortars going up higher and higher until they look as though they were clear up among the stars. . . . Some of them burst high in the air scattering pieces of shell in every direction and . . . dealing death to the inhabitants; others do not burst until after they strike, and then we can hear the crash as the shell goes down through the houses. . . . Our pickets are getting to be quite sociable with the enemy; it is quite a common occurrence for them to meet half way without arms to drink a cup of coffee together, and have a long talk over matters and things in general.*

Food was becoming scarcer every day. The one item that was in fairly good supply was peas. Soldiers began eating bread made of ground peas, and the civilians soon followed suit. Women went into the fields and gathered cane shoots to cook for their children. They also collected blackberries, tree buds, and weeds, mixing them with half-ripe peaches to make a stew. Like many others, Lucy McRae ate mule meat, which "tasted right good, having been cooked nicely." Wheat bread had become a rarity, and the adults drank coffee made from sweet potatoes. Mrs. Lord wrote that she and her five children would "have been badly off," if it had not been for "the kindness" of a lieutenant who sold her a gallon of molasses for six dollars.

By early June the summer sun was beating down into the streets of Vicksburg. People began dipping water from trenches and mud holes; others with underground cisterns sold fresh water by the bucketful to those who could afford it. In the midst of the searing heat the daily shelling went on. Mary Loughborough told in her diary of her daughter's distress when the shells fell near her cave: "She ran to me breathless, hiding her head in my dress without a word; then cautiously looking out . . . would say: "Oh, mamma was it a mortar tell?"

That same day a little black girl was mangled by the explosion of a shell she had found in her yard; the arm of a three-year-old boy was shattered by a shell fragment, and a young girl was killed by a mortar shell as she ran from her house to seek shelter in a cave. And William Lord Jr. barely escaped death from a spent shell that passed so near the top of his head that it singed his hair. Fortunately, he had stooped down for a moment to pick up something from the ground. After the charge had been carefully withdrawn by his soldier friends from Missouri, he added the shell to his collection of "war treasures."

The officer husband of Mary Loughborough grew so concerned about her safety in the town that he moved her and their daughter to a safer place—to the front. Mary described her new shelter:

> A low, long room, cut into the hillside and shaded by the growth of forest trees around was . . . our future home. What a pleasant place, after the close little cave in the city! . . . I took possession delightedly. A blanket, hung across the centre, made us two good-sized rooms: the front room, with a piece of carpet laid down to protect us from the dampness of the floor, and two or three chairs, formed our little parlor; and the back room, quiet and retired, the bedroom. We had our tent fly drawn over the front, making a very pleasant veranda. . . . We were in the first line of hills back of the heights that were fortified.

Now and then, the officers in the surrounding breastworks would send the young mother and her little girl some precious food items: two large yellow June apples, four slices of ham. One day a friend brought her some fruit. While the adults were conversing, Mary's two-year-old daughter quietly ate it. When she had nearly finished all of it, she turned around with a bright and well-satisfied face and said: "Mamma, it's so dood!" She had eaten her mother's portion as well. The soldiers, meanwhile, were reduced to half rations—flour or meal enough to furnish two biscuits in two days. Many ate it all at once and fasted the next day.

Back in town, Mrs. Lord and her children were still in their cave, still clinging to the hope that Vicksburg might be relieved in a few days. A messenger had brought a dispatch to General Pemberton, promising relief by General Johnston's army. She wrote on June 23: "To-morrow and the next day we will listen so eagerly for the sound of battle—may the Almighty who can save by many or by few fight for us and give us victory."

But relief did not come to the embattled city. Two days later, on June 25, Dora Miller wrote in her journal:

> *A horrible day. The most horrible yet to me, because I've lost my nerve. We were all in the cellar when a shell came tearing through the roof, burst upstairs, tore up that room and the pieces came through both floors down into the cellar. This was tangible proof the cellar was no protection from them. On the heels of this came . . . Martha . . . horror-stricken to tell us the black girl . . . had her arm taken off by a shell. For the first time I quailed. . . . Every night I had laid down expecting death, and every morning rose to the same prospect, without being unnerved. . . . But now I first seemed to realize that something worse than death might come: I might be crippled and not killed. Life, without all one's powers and limbs, was a thought that broke down my courage.*

Another accident cast a gloom over Mary Loughborough and her daughter. A soldier named Henry had befriended her little girl, bringing her flowers on one visit, an apple on another, and even a young mockingbird. Seeing him riding the general's handsome horse to water it one morning, she called attention to him, saying: "O mamma, look at Henry's horse, how he plays!" Soon after, he came down the hill with an unexploded shrapnel shell in his hand. A few moments later there was a quick explosion, and Henry, with his hands torn off his wrist and a wound in his head, cried; "Where are you, boys? Oh, I am hurt. God have mercy!" The little girl clung to her mother's dress, saying: "O mamma, poor Henry's killed! Now he'll die, mamma. Oh, poor Henry!" Sadly her mother carried her away from the painful sight.

In her cave in Vicksburg, Mrs. Lord was beginning to lose hope. On June 28, she wrote: "Still in this dreary cave. Who would have believed that we could have born such a life for five weeks? The siege has lasted 42 days and yet no relief—every day this week we have waited for the sound of General Johnston's guns, but in vain." Her once proud and prosperous city by now had the appearance of having been visited "by a terrible scourge."

Confederate Sergeant Willie Tunnard, an infantryman from Louisiana, described what Vicksburg looked like during the last week of the siege:

Palatial residences were crumbling into ruins, the walks torn up by mortar shells. . . . Fences were torn down and houses pulled to pieces for fire-wood. . . . Dogs howled through the streets at nights; cats screamed their hideous cries; an army of rats, seeking food, would scamper around your very feet and across the streets and over the pavements. Lice and filth covered the bodies of the soldiers. Delicate women and children, with pale, care-worn and hunger-pinched features peered at the passer-by with wistful eyes from the caves in the hillsides.

Back in her ravine near the front line, Mary Loughborough was sick; her daughter swung in her hammock, with a low-grade fever flushing her face. A soldier brought a little jaybird as a plaything for the child. Her daughter played with it a little while, then wearily turned away. "Miss Mary," said her servant, "she is hungry; let me make her some soup from the bird." Her mother halfheartedly consented. She wrote in her diary: "The next time she appeared, it was with a cup of soup, and a little plate on which lay the white meat of the poor little bird."

As hunger spread in Vicksburg, several observers noted that dogs— which earlier had run through the streets howling during every bombardment—had all but disappeared, along with cats. Dora Miller wrote on July 3: "Today we are down in the cellar again; provisions so nearly gone . . . that a few more days will bring us to starvation. Martha says rats are hanging dressed in the market for sale with mule-meat; there is nothing else."

Sixteen-year-old Theodore Upson had come down the river with his Indiana regiment to block the Confederate troops of General Johnston, who was trying to break the siege of Vicksburg. He wrote to his parents on July 3:

The regiment was sent out yesterday on a scout to see if there were any Confederate forces on this side of Black River. We captured a few prisoners and some deserters from Vicksburg who say their army there are very short of provision, but we found no large force of the enemy and came back that night, tired, hungry, and mad. We can hear the firing all the time and at night see the immense shells that our mortar guns are dropping into Vicksburg by hundreds night and day. . . . Last evening we heard that negotiations were in progress for the surrender of Vicksburg.

At five o'clock on the afternoon of July 3 the last shot rang out from the river batteries. That night rockets exploded over the city in a myriad of holiday colors. Just before daybreak on July 4, a few rattling shots were heard along the lines. Then, when the sun came up, there was only silence. General Pemberton, a Pennsylvanian by birth, surrendered with his thirty-one thousand Confederate troops on the nation's birthday. "I know my people," he told his staff. "I know we can get better terms from them on the Fourth of July than on any other day of the year." It was the forty-eighth day of the siege.

Twelve-year-old Fred Grant was present when General Grant was handed a note from a messenger. He observed:

In a moment my father gave a sigh of relief and said calmly, "Vicksburg has surrendered.". . . In this way I was the first to hear . . . the announcement. I felt enthused, going rapidly from my father's tent to tell the news to my kind friends of the cavalry escort. . . . They did now know that from that time on the Mississippi would "flow unvexed to the sea."

Wrote a disheartened Mrs. Lord in her journal:

About 1/2 past 8 o'clock, before I was dressed, Mr. Lord came into the cave, pale as death and with such a look of agony on his face, as I would wish never to see again, said Maggie take the children home directly, the town is surrendered, and the Yankee army will enter at 10 o'clock. . . . I was speechless with grief, no one spoke, even the poor children were silent. . . . As I started up the hill with the children, the tears began to flow and all the weary way home, I wept incessantly. . . . At last we reached the house, and such a scene of desolation you can hardly imagine. The dressing room was in ruins, the end where the fireplace had been was blown entirely out. The nursery uninhabitable, a hole deep almost as a cistern in the middle of the floor, every room in the house injured and scarcely a window left whole, but this is a small matter. . . . You can imagine our feelings when the U.S. Army entered, their banners flying and their hateful tunes sounding in our ears. Every house was closed . . . filled with weeping inmates and mourning hearts. You may be sure none of us raised our eyes to see the flag of the enemy in the place where our own had so proudly and defiantly waved so long.

The tattered and starving soldiers who had defended Vicksburg stacked their arms and waited to be released to the Confederate lines. "The drummer boy of a Tennessee regiment rather than give up his drum gave it to my brother" remembered little Lucy McRae. "No word of exultation was uttered to irritate the feelings of the prisoners," wrote Willie Tunnard with some wonderment.

One of Grant's first acts was to feed the people of Vicksburg. As the Confederate soldiers began to line up for their final muster they carried in their knapsacks for the first time in many months ample rations, "pressed upon them by a hospitable and admiring foe," observed William Lord Jr.

At the wharves down by the riverfront, Theodore Upson was unloading supplies from the steamboats: "It takes a lot of provisions to feed all of our troops," he wrote home to Indiana, "to say nothing of the 30,000 Johnnys who have been hungry so long. It will take a lot to fill them up. I should think those fellows would be glad to quit and some of them did say they wished the war was over."

The people of Vicksburg—men, women and children—filed out of their caves to pick up the pieces of their shattered homes and lives, with memories of the siege that would stay with them forever. "I do not think a child could have passed through what I did and have forgotten it," wrote Lucy McRae years later, when she was a married woman. All that Lucy and her fellow citizens could call upon now was their fierce pride.

A few weeks after the Yankees moved in, the five Lord children left Vicksburg with their parents, going first to Mobile, Alabama, and then to Charleston, South Carolina. When Sherman's troops captured Charleston, they fled inland to Winnsboro. After the war, their father returned to Vicksburg to become pastor of a newly constructed church.

Mary Loughborough and her daughter were denied permission to accompany her husband when the Confederate prisoners left Vicksburg bound for Mobile. She and a number of other women traveled up the Mississippi River, which was now completely under the control of Federal troops, and found a home in St. Louis, Missouri. One day she showed her Vicksburg journal to a friend, who urged her to have it published. *My Cave Life in Vicksburg*, printed first in 1864 in New York, was well received by Northern readers, even though she dedicated her book to her rebel husband, now back on active duty with the Confederate army.

The Fourth of July would not be celebrated again in Vicksburg for eighty-one years. In the summer of 1945, at the end of World War II, the proud people of that city finally accepted a decision made almost a hundred years before: They belonged to the United States. Throughout the day and into the night, the city celebrated the birthday of their nation— invincible *and* indivisible.

— 7 —

MY HEART ACHES FOR THOSE POOR WRETCHES

ON FEBRUARY 15, 1864, a trainload of Union prisoners stopped at a clearing near a stretch of dense pinewood and vine-tangled swamps, some sixty miles southwest of Macon, Georgia.

> *We were taken from the railroad cars to an open piece of ground. . . . Looking eastward about a quarter of a mile we could see an immense stockade. . . . The sight near the gate of a pile of dead . . . their faces black with grime and pinched with pain and hunger . . . gave us some idea that a like fate awaited us inside. . . . The gates swung open on their massive iron hinges and we marched in. . . . At various places [we saw] different instruments of torture: stocks, thumb screws, barbed iron collars, shackles, ball and chain. Our prison keepers seemed to handle them with familiarity.*

The voice is that of Michael Dougherty, from the Thirteenth Pennsylvania Cavalry, who was captured at age sixteen by General Lee's army in Virginia in October 1863. His comrades were among the thirteen thousand men who died at the Confederate prison camp of Andersonville and were buried there in mass graves. A Georgia girl, Eliza F. Andrews, age seventeen, was allowed to visit the camp and never forgot what she saw:

> *My heart aches for those poor wretches, Yankees though they are, and I am afraid God will suffer some terrible retribution to fall upon us for letting such things happen. If the Yankees should ever come to southwest Georgia and go to Anderson and see the graves there, God have mercy on the land!*

The retribution came on November 10, 1865, when Captain Henri Wirz, the commandant of Andersonville, was hung by the neck in Washington, D.C. He had been found guilty by a military court of a long list of crimes designed "to injure the health and destroy the lives" of some forty-five thousand Union soldiers who had been prisoners at Andersonville during the time he was in charge. Wrote the judge advocate: "The widespread sacrifice of life . . . was accomplished slowly and deliberately by packing upwards of 30,000 men, like cattle in a fetid pen—there to die for need of air to breathe, for want of ground on which to lie, from lack of shelter from sun and rain, and from the slow agonizing process of starvation." There were also specific acts of brutality—hunting men down with dogs, confining them in the stocks, cruelly beating and murdering them—of which Wirz was found personally guilty.

Among the one hundred fifty eyewitnesses called for the trial was Billy Bates from Ohio, who was only fifteen years old when he first arrived in Andersonville. As prisoners began pouring into the yet unfinished stockades, each inmate's daily ration was reduced to a teaspoon of salt, three tablespoons of beans, and half a pint of unsifted cornmeal. A filthy creek served as source of drinking water and sewer. Most prisoners lived in holes scratched into the ground. Any man caught closer than fifteen feet to the stockade, in the Dead Line, was shot. Undaunted, Billy Bates and his friend Dick King, age seventeen, charted their map for survival:

> Our reason convinced us that we must not sit down in idleness and despair. Our existence depended on mental and bodily exercise and the hope of escape. So we commenced a systematic visitation of all new arrivals; discussed all imaginable plans for getting away; roused the hypochondriacs and actually provoked quarrels with some of the most gloomy for the sole purpose of awakening a spark of interest in their present lives. We soon found that this was good for them and greatly benefited ourselves. Several schemes for tunneling and escaping were commenced.

The commandant learned about their plans from an informer. He arrested the two teenagers and put them in a chain gang. To teach Billy Bates a lesson, his thumbs were tied together with a cord. He was then suspended by a rope that ran up to a beam over the gateway in plain view of everyone in the camp. A compassionate fellow prisoner gave the boy some water from an old slop pan and was promptly shot dead by an irate Wirz, who then turned to Billy and shot him twice in the left thigh and leg. A mob gathered; the guards ran the commandant off to safety. The prisoners cut the boy down and took care of him as best they could. His friend Dick divided his rations with Billy and nursed him back to health, keeping his wounds wet day and night to prevent the onset of gangrene.

After Billy recovered, the two boys spent nearly eight months digging an eighteen- by twenty-four-inch tunnel that reached beyond the prison wall. It was barely large enough to crawl through.

On the night of March 2, 1864—thirteen months after they had been marched into the prison pen—the two boys escaped. They traveled at night, hid during the day, and foraged for subsistence, assisted by some black ex-slaves. Three weeks later they reached the Union lines near Bridgeport, Alabama. Billy Bates weighed sixty pounds, and his friend Dick weighed sixty-four pounds when they were received by President Lincoln at the White House on April 28, 1864. They told him all they knew about the horrors of Andersonville. When they had finished, the president sprang to his feet and exclaimed, "My God, when will this accursed thing end?"

Another teenage prisoner was not as lucky in his attempt to escape. One of his fellow prisoners, Thomas W. Way, testified at the Wirz trial:

He was a young fellow . . . I knew him by the name of Fred. He was about 17 years old. When we heard the dogs coming, I and another prisoner who was with me, being old hands, climbed a tree. He tried to do so, but he had not got up when the hounds caught him by the foot and pulled him down; and in less than three minutes he was torn all to pieces.

The worst was yet to come: Michael Dougherty and another teenage cavalryman, John McElroy, were in Andersonville when its population reached thirty-three thousand in late spring 1864. The camp had been "designed" to hold only ten thousand men. One out of every three prisoners died within one month of arriving. On May 8, Michael Dougherty wrote:

I have lain on the battle field . . . surrounded with dead and dying and listening to the agonizing cries of the wounded, but it is nothing compared to this den of misery and woe, the memory of which will be ever present to those who have experienced it. Nearly one-half of the old prisoners are dead and nearly all of those living are prostrated with scurvy and gangrene. . . . Unless one was there, it is hard for the mind to grasp the magnitude of this hell on earth.

His diary entry a few days later reads:

There are millions and millions of all kinds of vermin here, flies, bugs, maggots and lice, some of them as large as spiders. If they once get the best of you, you are a goner. A great many of the prisoners are hopelessly crazy, starvation, disease and vermin being the cause. . . . I am somewhat crippled, myself, but I manage to try and wash and keep clean, that is the principal thing. One hundred have died within the last 24 hours.

Observed his fellow prisoner, seventeen-year-old John McElroy from Illinois:

I can recall few or no instances where a large strong "hearty" man lived through more than a few months of imprisonment. The survivors were invariably youths at the verge of manhood, slender, quick, active, medium-statured fellows, of a cheerful temperament.

Both Michael Dougherty and John McElroy fit this description. They vowed to keep up their spirits as long as there was a spark of life left in them. McElroy recalled how they managed to spend their time—"a time that moved with leaden feet."

Card playing had sufficed to pass the hours away at first, but our cards soon wore out. . . . My chum Andrews and I constructed a set of chessmen. . . . We found a soft white root in the swamp. A boy near us had a tolerably sharp pocket knife for the use of which a couple of hours each day we gave a few spoonful of meal. The shapes that we made for pieces and pawns were crude, but sufficiently distinct for identification. We blackened one set with pitch-pine soot, found a piece of plank for a board . . . and so were fitted out with what served until our release to distract our attention from much of the surrounding misery.

Newcomers who still had money and cards gambled as long as their means lasted. Those who had books read them until the bindings fell apart. John McElroy met a boy who had brought a copy of Gray's *Anatomy* into prison. He borrowed the book and tackled it with such enthusiasm that before long he had a fair knowledge of the rudiments of physiology.

Those who had paper and pen and ink tried to keep journals, but most gave up after being in prison for a few weeks. Michael Dougherty was an exception. He kept a diary for fifteen months. On June 8, 1864, he wrote:

Got a diary from one of the new prisoners; glad of it, for mine was almost full. He said I was doing something he could not do. Well, I commenced it and it comes naturally to me now, besides it occupies my mind and gives me some exercise twice a day going from one end to the prison to the other hunting up news. I will soon have to look out for a new pencil. This is the fourth piece and it is very short.

One of the best purveyors of information in the camp was a bright, blue-eyed, fair-haired drummer boy who had been captured in action in the Shenandoah Valley. Ransom Powell was only thirteen years old and wore a jaunty gold-laced crimson cap, earning him the nickname Red Cap. Shortly after Captain Wirz assumed command, he took the drummer boy into his office as orderly, a point that was made in the captain's defense at his trial. Red Cap was one of the most popular persons in prison: He kept his ears open to the conversation of the rebel officers around him and frequently secured permission to visit the interior of the stockade, where he would communicate to his fellow prisoners all that he had heard.

"It seemed utterly shameful that men, calling themselves soldiers, should make war on such a tender boy and drag him off to prison," wrote John McElroy. "But no six-footer had a more soldierly heart than little Red Cap, and none was more loyal to the cause. . . . He was a good observer and told his tale with boyish fervor." He survived the war with his spirit unbroken.

The teenage prisoners who managed to survive did their best to keep body and soul together. In the midst of sickness and death they found solace in the company of a little band of devout Union soldiers who would take their station in some part of the stockade—a different one every time—and sing some old familiar hymn. In a few minutes they would have an attentive audience of thousands for their short but spirited sermons. They also tried, as best they could, to minister to the sick and dying.

The only clergyman who came into the stockade from the outside was a Catholic priest, Father Hamilton. "I certainly believe he is a true Christian," wrote Michael Dougherty in his prison diary. "He ministers to the Catholics and Protestants alike." John McElroy noted that the priest was "unwearied in his attention to the sick. . . . The whole day he could be seen moving around the prison attending those who needed consolation."

But with each succeeding summer day, conditions grew worse in Andersonville. On July 3, Michael Dougherty wrote:

> *We cannot live long on the quantities of rations we have been getting. Thinking of our friends at home who are preparing to celebrate the Nation's birthday of freedom to-morrow; they do not imagine the conditions of us poor sufferers in this acursed place.*

On the Fourth of July, 1864, there were no rations of any kind for the prisoners at Andersonville. John McElroy thought of food all day. At night he dreamed he was at a banquet at a fancy restaurant in St. Louis that he had once attended as a boy:

> *I saw the tables gleaming with cut glass and silver, the buffets with wine and fruits. . . . I revelled in all the dainties and dishes on the bill of fare, calling for everything . . . just to see what each was like and to be able to say afterward that I had partaken of it. All these bewildering delights . . . would*

dance through my somnolent brain. Then I would awake to find myself, a
half-starved, half-naked, vermin-eaten wretch, crouching in a hole in the
ground, waiting for my keepers to fling me a chunk of corn bread.

"Rations, one pint of meal, two spoonfuls of beans and two ounces of
bacon," noted Michael Dougherty in his journal the next day. "The prisoners are almost crazy with hunger." A diary entry a week later reads:

The number of deaths in camp reached its highest mark yesterday, one hun-
dred and eighty-five having died. I don't wonder as everything is composed
of dirt and filth; the stench from the swamp is sickening and the water full
of maggots and all kinds of vermin, which we must use or die of thirst. . . .
We are suffering very much from heat, as we have no shelter of any kind to
protect us from the scorching sun; we are almost all barefooted and hatless.

John McElroy gave a graphic description of the way his own clothes
dropped off piece by piece, "like petals from the last rose of summer":

First my boots fell into ruin. . . . Then part of the underclothing retired from
service. The jacket and the vest followed, their end being hastened by having
the best portions taken to patch up the pantaloons which kept giving out at the
most embarrassing places. . . . The clothing upon the upper part of my body
had been reduced to the remains of a knit undershirt. . . . Wherever holes were,
the sun had burned my back, breast and shoulders deeply black. The parts cov-
ered by the threads and fragments forming the boundaries of the holes were
still white. Whenever I put my shirt off to wash it . . . my skin showed a fine
lace pattern in black and white that was . . . the subject of countless jokes.

Father Hamilton, who continued to minister to the soldiers in Andersonville in the summer heat, saw a prisoner who had no garment left but
his shirt. To make it cover him better in the scorching sun, he put his legs
into the sleeves and tied the tail around his neck. The other prisoners
teased him so much about his appearance that he became despondent.
One day he deliberately stepped over the Dead Line and stood there until a guard shot him. Other prisoners who were stark naked but intent on
their survival burrowed into the ground like moles to protect themselves
from the scorching sun.
   John McElroy kept up his clothing by stealing cotton mealsacks and
tearing them in two. Wrote he: "The cotton cloth gained in this way was
used for patching. If a boy could succeed in beating the rebels out of
enough of it, he could fabricate himself a shirt or a pair of pantaloons."
   Thread was obtained in the same way—from sacks—with the threads
carefully raveled out. Most of the needles for the handiwork were manu-

factured from bones. A piece of bone was carefully rubbed down upon a brick; then an eye was laboriously worked through it with a piece of wire. "I do not think any Plains Indians exceeded us in the patience with which we worked away at these minutiae of life's needs," John McElroy remembered. "Of course, the most common source of clothing was the dead. No body was carried out with any clothing on it that could be of service to the survivors."

On August 24, 1864—the date of the greatest number of deaths in Andersonville—one Union soldier died every ten minutes. There were probably twelve thousand seriously ill in the camp at any given time during that month. Every morning after roll call, thousands of sick men gathered at the south gate for some medical relief. Some were admitted into the prison hospital. This was a dubious privilege since the prison records show that among the "registered patients" in Andersonville the mortality rate had reached seventy-five percent.

But even in the midst of the worst suffering, compassion did not die. John McElroy saw an "admirable illustration" when visiting a comrade in the hospital:

> The U.S. sloop Water Witch *had recently been captured.... One of her boys, a bright, handsome little fellow of about fifteen, had lost one of his arms in the fight. He was brought into the hospital and an older fellow ... was allowed to accompany him and nurse him.... They found a shady nook in one corner, and any moment one looked ... one could see the old tar hard at work. Now he was dressing the wound as deftly and gently as a mother caring for her new-born babe; now he was trying to concoct some relish out of the materials he could beg or steal from the Quartermaster; now trying to arrange the shade of the bed of pine leaves in a more comfortable manner; now repairing or washing [the boy's] clothes.*

One morning in August when the situation in the pen was at its worst, the prisoners were surprised to discover that during the night a large spring had burst out on the north side of the camp. It poured out pure sweet water in a seemingly exhaustless quantity. The prisoners promptly named it Providence Spring. "It seemed as truly a ... miracle as when Moses' rod smote the parched earth in Sinai's desert waste, and the living waters gushed forth," wrote John McElroy. From now on, every morning, shortly after daybreak, thousands of men would stand in line, waiting to fill their cups and cans with clean water. The spring would save many a life in Andersonville.

On the evening of September 6, 1864, John McElroy heard the welcome news that he would be among twenty thousand prisoners to be exchanged in Savannah. He and his comrades would leave Andersonville

the very next day. "The excitement that this news produced was inde-
scribable," he remembered. "Boys sang and shouted as if in a delirium. It
had come at last—that which we had so longed for, wished for, prayed
for, dreamed of."

The next morning, John and his friend Andrews picked up their well-
worn blanket, their tattered overcoat, their chessmen and board, and
their little black can and spoon made of hoop-iron and bade farewell to
the hole in the ground that had been their home for eight long months.
McElroy's feet were still in miserable condition from the lacerations he
had received in an earlier attempt to escape, so he took a tent pole in
hand and hobbled away.

Michael Dougherty was *not* among the prisoners selected for exchange. A week earlier he had been taken to the prison hospital at Andersonville "completely used up with rheumatism." A few days before he
gave up writing because of the pain, he had scribbled in his diary, "I will
try and keep up my courage and trust in God to get me out of this place."

There were fifteen wards in the hospital, twelve tents in each ward,
each tent containing twelve men—lying on the floor, without any quilts
or blankets. One of Michael's tentmates died the first day, and six more
succumbed within a month of his arrival. But Michael Dougherty was a
survivor. His diary entry on September 16 reads: "Have been in here over
two weeks; the doctor says I will pull through all right." And on September 28: "One month in the hospital today; our rations are a little better
here than in the pen."

Father Hamilton and two Sisters of Charity who attended to the sick in
the prison hospital thought Michael was "too young to be in the army."
They made a special effort to visit him every day and to bring him
"something nice to eat." The priest had sold some property in Savannah
and had bought sixteen hundred barrels of flour so that the sick among
the Union prisoners would get some wheat bread. On occasion he would
bring Michael a piece of cold roast beef and a slice of bread and butter.
On the youth's first "anniversary" as a prisoner, Father Hamilton
brought him an undershirt. "He said I looked better," Dougherty wrote
in his diary on October 11.

That week Private William Smith got *his* first glimpse of Andersonville.
At age fifteen, when he was barely measuring up to the required soldiers'
height of five feet six inches, he had enlisted in the Fourteenth Illinois Infantry Regiment. Now he was a Union prisoner packed in an overcrowded train of the Macon and Albany Railroad line. On that train he
had met "one of the scrawniest, raggedest, and most filthy Union soldier[s]" who had escaped from prison and been recaptured.

"Comrades," this skeleton had said, "you will not believe my story, but
I tell you now you are all going to hell." Like his fellow passengers in the

crowded box car, young William Smith entirely discredited the news the man told them of Andersonville's horrors. "I thought he was either a great liar or a deranged person who had been wandering around among the swamps and pine forests until he had become nearly starved and naked." But the reality William Smith encountered was worse than the stranger's tale:

> *On our way to the pen we saw four ragged skeleton-looking Union prisoners confined in stocks, with hands, feet and neck securely fastened. As they lay there motionless . . . they were in appearance much like the poor fellow [on the train], and looked as if they might be dead. . . . At the south gate we passed a brush shelter. Lying on the ground . . . we counted over twenty emaciated, blackened human forms. Most of them were covered from head to foot with sores . . . and entirely destitute of clothing. . . . As we entered the inner stockade [we saw] fifteen more shroudless dead, covered with filth and vermin. . . . The great mass of gaunt, unnatural-looking beings, soot-begrimed, and clad in filthy tatters that we saw stalking about inside this pen looked . . . as if they belonged to a world of lost spirits. . . . As for myself, I never felt so utterly depressed, crushed and God-forsaken in all my life.*

In October 1864, prison records showed the highest death rates in the history of Andersonville: One in every two prisoners died. William Smith managed to survive. The morning after their arrival in the pen he and six young comrades, all under the age of eighteen, began to assess the situation coolly and resolutely. "One opinion prevailed," he remembered, "that no man could live to get out of that prison who should abandon hope or loose his grit . . . We pledged to keep our persons as clean as possible, and to stand by each other in all that might befall us—a vow that was never broken."

That morning, the seven boys began to build their common shelter in their "Wirz Hotel." They got hold of three small tent stakes and four pegs, then whittled out some little wooden pins with which they pinned together the two blankets they owned. Once up, these provided protection from the sun during the day and from the damp dews and chilly air in the night. They slept on their sides "spoon fashion." When one got tired and turned over, all the rest had to turn with him; lying on the hard ground made this movement necessary about every half hour.

When rations came in the evening, they kept back a little for breakfast. During the day, they made out with the water from Providence Spring as best they could. Willie Smith traded three of his brass buttons with a prison guard for some coarse salt to improve his corn mush, and some soup bones with a new group of prisoners who enroute to Andersonville from Meridian, Mississippi, had been fed with the offal from a slaughterhouse. "I made dumplings out of my meal ration by working it into a stiff dough and rolling it into little balls," he wrote. "These little marbles, cooked with the broken up soup bones . . . tasted so *delicious* . . . superior to anything I had ever eaten."

Their ration wagon, which came around in the evening, was also Andersonville's hearse, used to haul the dead from the gates to their place of burial. On evenings when the prisoners drew meat, which was generally about two to three ounces of boiled beef, there were lively trading scenes in the camp. The men who had lost their teeth from scurvy wanted soup, mush or meal in exchange for their hard cornbread. Those suffering from dysentery wanted a soup bone or soup. "Thus the trading was carried on until each man had done the best he could do for himself," William Smith observed.

In the prison hospital, meanwhile, Michael Dougherty had suffered another attack of severe rheumatism. In mid-November, Father Hamilton brought him a bottle of milk—the first milk he had tasted in thirteen months. A couple of weeks later, one of the doctor's dogs strayed into the tent he shared with eleven other prisoners; one of the men threw a blanket over the dog and killed him. "He ate part of it and said it was elegant," noted Michael in his diary. "He buried the entrails, but one of the other poor fellows dug them up, cooked and ate them."

The last entry in Dougherty's prison diary was on December 10, 1864: "I feel no better. My diary is full; it is too bad but [I] cannot get any more. Goodbye all; I did not think I would hold out so long when I commenced."

Christmas Eve came two weeks later. William Smith recalled that night as "the most horrible experience in all my prison life." Each of the boys drew a half pint of cold mush and two tablespoonsful of vinegar, made out of sorghum molasses, intended as an antidote for scurvy. As night came, a cold rain set in; it soon turned to sleet. He and his comrades lay on the ground, "spooning as closely as if glued together with the mud" in order to keep warm.

On Christmas morning the sun appeared and thawed everything out. While they were constructing mud huts out of the soggy clay and digging out more "spooning holes," the boys talked of their families at home and dreamed of filled stockings, rich presents, roasted turkeys, mince pies, and fruitcakes. When their Christmas dinner was brought in the afternoon, each prisoner received three ounces of cold beef and a chunk of coarse unsalted cornmeal "about two inches thick and some four inches square."

The sun . . . was rapidly sinking in the west, the December air becoming quite chilly. We all needed something with which to warm us up, so in the absence of any warm rations to eat or drink we improved our Christmas repast somewhat by removing the thick upper and lower crusts from our corn bread, which we toasted brown by our little fires, broke up into small bits, and in our can or bucket each made himself a quart of smoking hot "Andersonville" coffee. This we drank and ate, grounds and all, and I venture that no tea, or chocolate, or coffee drank in any Northern home that Christmas evening was relished by us shivering prisoners, huddled around our little fires sipping our warm beverage out of our black buckets, cups, wooden plates, or cowhorns, as did our improvised Andersonville coffee. All the while [we were] slowly nibbling our cold beef and corn bread so as to make them last as long as possible, and the meanwhile talking over the probable features of Christmas dinners at our homes and wondering if we should ever live to join our dear ones again on these festive occasions.

After they had made the most of their Christmas rations, William Smith and his comrades lay down in their "spooning hole," covered with their old blankets, and found themselves much more comfortable than on the night before. In the days to come they collected pine needles that eventually covered about half an inch of the bottom of their hole. This made a decided improvement over the bare ground for sleep on a winter night.

In January 1865, William Smith came down with a severe case of scurvy. His comrades had to draw and prepare his rations for him. He never forgot their compassion: "I was the youngest by several years of my mess, and they all treated me with the same tender care . . . they would have extended toward a younger brother," he wrote later. His condition grew progressively worse in February and March, when neither his shirt nor bandage could be removed. But his spirit never faltered.

The prisoners from Andersonville did not hear about the collapse of the Confederacy until mid-April 1865. On April 20, 1865, Smith and the six other boys who had been his constant companions in Andersonville marched out of prison as free men—he with a stick as his cane, his feet and ankle bandaged with rags. "As we passed through those old prison gates," he remembered, "I believe we emerged from one of the most horrible, ghastly places the world has ever known."

But his sense of humor had not deserted him. Wrote he:

Before taking leave of this anti-fat sanatorium I must say a word in favor of its proprietor. He never ran a bar in connection with his hotel, nor did I ever see a drunken border or a drop of intoxicating liquor on the premises while I was his guest. Still I could not recommend his bill of fare or lodging.

The sick in the hospital of Andersonville were the last to be released. On April 23, Michael Dougherty found himself in Vicksburg boarding the riverboat *Sultana*. He and some twenty-two hundred other ex-prisoners from Andersonville were destined for St. Louis, Missouri. Two Sisters of Charity accompanied the men.

Three days after their departure from Vicksburg the boat reached Memphis, Tennessee, where a quantity of sugar, which had served as a ballast, was unloaded. After dark, the *Sultana* started on its final trip up the river. Around 4 A.M. the next morning, there was a terrific explosion: One of the four boilers had burst, and the flying pieces almost cut the vessel in two. In a short time, the entire ship was engulfed in flames—the cabins burned like tinder. Hundreds of soldiers drowned; among the dead was a courageous nun who had put her life on the line to calm some of the frantic men who "were fighting like demons" in the water. Michael Dougherty survived—"more dead than alive . . . crippled with rheumatism and scurvy, weighing less than one hundred pounds."

He was the sole survivor of 127 members of his regiment who had been prisoners in Andersonville.

— 8 —

THEY CAME BURNING
ATLANTA TODAY

O N A HOT AND HUMID DAY IN JULY 1864, Carrie Berry, a ten-year-old girl from Atlanta, began a diary that chronicled the fate of her city in the wake of General Sherman's approaching army:

> We can hear the canons and muskets very plane, but the shells we dread.
> One has busted under the dining room which frightened us very much. One
> passed through the smokehouse and a piece hit the top of the house and fell
> through. . . . We stay very close to the cellar when they are shelling.

Atlanta by that time was filled with refugees who came in wagons and on foot, mostly old men, young boys, anxious women, and young girls in sunbonnets and faded calico. They had fled from their up-country farms and villages. City parks were filled with hospital tents smelling of disinfectants and the stench of gangrene. Trains brought loads of sick and wounded Confederate soldiers into town—many of them dying.

By mid-July, many residents of Atlanta who had relatives in southwest Georgia, in areas considered "safe," were leaving the city. Among them were Mary S. Mallard and her two young children, Mary, age six, and Charles, age four. In a letter from Augusta, dated July 18, 1864, she wrote:

> My dear Cousin,
> You have doubtless heard . . . that we have left Atlanta—at least for the
> present—and are now numbered among the numerous throngs of refugees.
> We had hoped to have remained longer in Atlanta, but when the order came
> to move all hospitals in a few hours and the enemy were reported as cross-
> ing the river within six miles of us, we thought we better move our furni-
> ture while we could get transportation.

We were detained in Atlanta by a serious accident which but for the mercy of God might have resulted fatally to some of us. . . . Descending a steep hill . . . something gave way about [our] cart and in a few moments we were all thrown out. The children were uninjured, saving bruises upon their faces but I was seriously injured, being bruised in every part of my body from my head to my feet. . . . I was quite a spectacle coming down on the cars, and often was asked, "Is you wounded?" I suppose they thought I was one of the unfortunate ones that had been caught between the lines when a battle was going on.

Four days later, the battle of Atlanta began for real. Confederate lines formed, fell back, reformed, attacked again, and ultimately withdrew. In little more than a week, a third of the Confederate forces were wiped out by Sherman's troops. The rest fell back into the city. The teenager Theodore Upson from Indiana wrote in his diary about his encounter with the Confederates:

On the 22 of July the Johnnys under their new General, Hood, came out from their works at Atlanta and jumped our boys. The first thing I knew they were all around us. I just slipped off my horse and dropped my revolver and sword belt right there. . . . We came along a dense thicket. I just dropped out and ran into it. . . . The balls cut through the bush all around me, but I was pretty safe in the hollow. . . . Then the shots came through the bush from both directions. . . . I could hear their yells as they went on either side of the thicket and was aufully afraid some of them would try to come through. But pretty soon they came running back in great disorder and the balls from our side came thicker than ever. By and by it quieted down.

Ensconced behind the ramparts of Atlanta, the Confederates expected Sherman's attack. Instead, he sealed off the city's supplies and waited. Federal guns began shelling the heavily fortified trenches and the city beyond. The siege went on for a month. Noble C. Williams, a young boy at the time, remembered how the residents prepared themselves for the ordeal:

Most of the citizens constructed . . . bombproofs, which were holes dug in the earth eight or ten feet deep . . . covered overhead with heavy beams which contained a covering of boards or tin to keep out the rain and then covered with earth from three to five feet deep. The entrance to the small door was dug out in the shape of the letter L [to prevent the entry of shell fragments].

In one of these cellars, Carrie Berry and her family sought refuge. Her diary entries during the month of August told how she, her pregnant mother, and a sickly sister coped with the daily shelling.

Carrie Berry (courtesy of the Atlanta History
Center)

Aug. 4. *The shells have been flying all day and we have stayed in the cellar.
Mama put me [to work] on some stockings this morning and I will try to
finish them before school commences.*

Aug. 5. *I knit all the morning. In the evening we had to run to Auntie's to
get in the cellar. We did not feel safe in our cellar, they fell so thick and fast.*

Aug. 6. *We have been in the cellar all day. . . .*

Aug. 9. *We have had to stay in the cellar all day the shells have been
falling so thick around the house. Two have fallen in the garden, but none of
us were hurt. . . .*

Aug. 11. *Mama has ben very buisy to day and I have been trying to help
her all I could. We had to go to the cellar often out of the shells. How I wish
the federals would quit shelling us so we could get out and get some fresh air.*

Aug. 14. *We had shells in abundance last night. We expected every one
would come through and hurt some of us but to our joy nothing on the lot
was hurt. . . . I dislike to stay in the cellar so close but our soldiers have to
stay in ditches.*

A few miles away, in the Union lines, Theodore Upson noted:

We are on the firing line again. . . . Our works are in an open field and the first thing we had to do after we came was to cover more deeply the graves of 3,000 Confederate dead which had been so hastily buried that they had become very offensive. Yesterday . . . some 20 or more peices of Artillery massed in our rear and began to shell the Confederate works over us. I think it was the hardest experience we have had. The roar of the guns was deafening . . . a number of us are partially deaf on account of it. . . . Just before we started we were issued a ration of whiskey but most of the boys refused to drink it saying if they were to be killed they wanted to die sober. Some way we all felt we were going into great danger.

One of the shells fired by the federal artillery units fell into Carrie Berry's garden and made a great hole. The bursting pieces flew into every direction—two fragments went into the dining room. Wrote Carrie on August 15, "I was never so frightened in my life. Zuie [her sister] was as pale as a corpse and I expect I was too. It did not take us long to fly to the cellar." The next night a large shell fragment came through her mother's bedroom and fell on one of the children's beds. Another shell destroyed her aunt's house nearby.

"We are very tired of living so," Carry confessed in her diary. But two days later, her optimism returned. "When I woke up this morning," she wrote on August 18, "I thought the hole town would be torn up. The cannons were so near and so loud but we soon found out that it was *our* guns so we have been very well content all day."

The respite from the federal artillery shells was short-lived. "The fate of Atlanta is still undecided," observed one of Carrie's neighbors on August 21. "It is said that about twenty lives have been destroyed by these terrible missiles since the enemy began to throw them into the city. . . . No one can tell but he may be the next victim."

That very day Carrie's father concluded that their cellar was not safe enough to withstand the continuing bombardment. The family had to move. Carrie wrote in her diary:

Aug. 22. I got up this morning and helped Mama pack up to move. We were glad to get out of our small cellar. We have a nice large cellar here where we can run as much as we please and enjoy it. Mama says that we make so much noise that she can't here the shells.

Aug. 23. We feel very comfortable since we have moved but Mama is fretted to death all the time for fear of fire. There is a fire in town nearly every day. I get so tired of being housed up all the time. The shells get worse and worse every day. O that something would stop them!

A week later, Carrie's wish was granted. On August 31, Sherman hurled most of his army against the Macon and Western Railroad south of the city, in one last attempt to break the Confederacy's resistance. It worked. George Drake, a teenage soldier from Illinois, wrote in a letter to his parents about the assault:

> *We moved around within two miles of the railroad. . . . At five o'clock [in the] evening we charged the rebbels. . . . The fort having 3 pieces of artillery made it pretty hard work. But we carried the works without mutch trouble and captured the three pieces of artillery. The rebs had them all ready loaded. Our boys turned them and fired them right into the rebel ranks. It mowed them down like grass before the reaper.*

On September 1, the Confederate troops left Atlanta. Carrie Berry wrote in her diary: "Directly after dinner Cousin Emma came down and told us that Atlanta would be evacuated this evening and we might look for the Federals in the morning. It was not long till the hole town found it out and such excitement there was." Sherman's troops entered the city the next day.

Wrote Carrie on September 2, 1864:

> *Every one has been trying to get all they could before the Federals come in the morning. They have been running with saques of meat, salt and to-bacco. They did act rediculous breaking open stores and robbing them. About twelve o'clock there were a few Federals came. . . . In about an hour the cavalry came. . . . We were all frightened. We were afraid they were go-ing to treat us badly. It was not long till the Infantry came in. They were or-derly and behaved very well. I think I shall like the Yankees very well.*

The boy Noble Williams had run upstairs in his home and hid under his bed when the Union soldiers came to town. But then he took heart and peered out of the window. Long columns of blue-coated soldiers pa-raded in front of his house. He remembered:

> *No sooner had they broken ranks than hundreds of soldiers' faces could be seen peering through the fence which separated the street from the garden, and as the grape arbor, filled with luscious grapes, appeared before their vi-sion, their mouths fairly watered and their stomachs seemed to contain an aching void that could only be filled by a speedy and vigorous assault upon them, which in less than five minutes was accomplished, greatly to the dam-age of both grapes and arbor. Perched as they were on every available inch of slat, they were reminders of a flock of hungry bluebirds.*

For Carrie Berry, the arrival of the Union soldiers meant two unexpected guests who came to her house "to beg for something to eat," and the sudden departure of her family's black servant girl, Mary. "The times are getting a little worse every day," she noted in her diary on September 7. "I will have to go to work to help Mama."

Among the thousands of Yankee soldiers that were pouring into Atlanta were two teenaged boys—Henry Campbell, a bugler from the Eighteenth Indiana Artillery Battery, and George Drake, from the Eighty-fifth Illinois Infantry Regiment. Wrote Henry Campbell in his diary:

I rode all over the city and took a good stare. . . . Shot and shell from our line have completely riddled the northwest part of the town. The yards of all the houses have "gopher holes" dug in them where the citizens took refuge during the fire. The continuous rattling of the long string of army wagons make it look like a busy city.

George Drake in a letter to his mother in Illinois, dated September 6, boasted that he, too, had seen "that grate city Atlanta that has been so mutch talk about. Atlanta is undoubtedly a pretty place and is well and thickly populated." A few days later, most of that population, including Carrie Berry's relatives and neighbors, left the city in response to Sherman's evacuation order. On September 5, the General had ordered all women whose husbands were in "rebel service" to leave the city in five days; the remainder were given fifteen days to pack and leave.

George Drake explained in a letter to his parents:

Those that have husbands in the rebel army have to go there [to the Confederate lines] and those that have not will take the oath [of allegiance to the United States of America]. They can stay [in Federally controlled territory] but have to go north of the Ohio River. These can stay that get [employment] from the government. This is simply because we have so long a transportation to keep up and because the rebbels are cutting our railroad every once in a while.

To Carrie Berry and her family the news "broke into all our [ar]rangements." Her diary entry on September 10 reads:

Every one I see seems sad. The citizens all think it is the most cruel thing to drive us from our home, but I think it would be so funny to move. Mama seems so troubled and she can't do any thing. Papa says he don't know where on earth to go.

Unidentified woman and two children (courtesy of the Eleanor S. Brockenbrough Library, Museum of the Confederacy, Richmond, Virginia)

The mayor of Atlanta and two councilmen sent an urgent letter to General Sherman that pictures the suffering his evacuation order would inflict on its residents:

Many poor women [here] are in [an] advanced state of pregnancy, others now have young children . . . whose husbands for the greater part are either in the army, prisoners, or dead. Others say "What are we to do? We have no house to go to, and no means to buy, build, or rent any; no parents, relatives, or friends?" This being so, how is it possible for the people still here—mostly women and children—to find any shelter? And how can they live through the winter in the woods—no shelter or sub-

sistence in the midst of strangers who know them not, and without the power to as-
sist them much if they are willing to do so?

Similar thoughts, no doubt, went through the minds of Carrie's parents as they began to pack their belongings. In the last moment, her father succeeded in finding employment that exempted him and his family from the move. Her diary on September 13 breaks the welcome news: "Papa got into business today and the rest of us went to work in earnest thinking that we will get to stay. I hope that we will. . . . Mama dislikes to move so much."

In the days to come, Carrie was kept busy with household tasks. She washed, ironed, cooked dinner, cleaned house, stitched a new dress for her sister, knitted socks, and sewed an apron for her mother. Soon it was time to say good-bye to her cousins Emma and Willie. "They are going off to-night for the north," reads her diary entry on September 26. "We all feel sorry to see [them] leave, for we feel so lonesome."

Little Willie had just learned to take three or four steps on his own before he and his mother joined the long line of Atlantans who were leaving town. Sixteen hundred whites—and an unknown number of blacks—packed what they could carry and fled the city in the last days of September.

October brought the first frost of the year, and the days grew dark and gloomy. Carrie's mood matched the weather. On the first Sunday of the month, she and a girlfriend took a walk through the city to see how the soldiers had destroyed some of the great antebellum homes. "It's a shame to see the fine houses torn down," she observed.

One of her favorite aunts was selling her things in preparation to go north. Carrie, who loved to sew and knit, spent days and evenings at her home, collecting quilt and doll scraps. "I am right sorry Auntie is going away," she lamented in her diary. "I don't blame her for I never would stay and be shelled again if I could get away, so we will be very sorry when she leaves."

During the third week of October the sun came out, and Carrie's mood improved. "This has been a beautiful day," she wrote in her diary on Sunday, October 23. "Mama and Papa took a walk this evening and they say that they never saw a place torn up like Atlanta is. Half of the houses are torn down."

The Federal troops that were stationed in Atlanta were making ready to move. George Drake, who had volunteered at age sixteen to join the Eighty-fifth Illinois Infantry Regiment, wrote his father a letter the day before his unit left the city:

I tell you father that I never regret the day that I enlisted for if I had staid
out of the army and went to school all the time I would not of learned half so
mutch. That is about war and men and the principles of some men.

For her part, Carrie Berry had grown fond of some of the Union soldiers who were quartered in her neighborhood. On October 30, she wrote in her diary:

They are all ready to move and it looks like every body is going to leave from here the way the soldiers are moving about. Our sargent left us this morning. We all were sorry to part with him. He has been a very good friend to us.

A few days later, on November 4, she fretted that "the Federals are going to have to leave Atlanta and we are afraid that we will have to leave, too." On November 7, she wrote, "Every body seems to be in confusion. The black wimmen are running around trying to get north for fear that the Rebels will come in and take them."

The Hundredth Indiana Infantry Regiment returned to Atlanta on November 8, having marched some 350 miles in the unsuccessful pursuit of Confederate General John Bell Hood. Theodore Upson wrote that night in his diary:

We have been tearing up some more Rail Road and utterly destroying evry thing in the City that can be of any use to the Armies of the South. There are rumors that we are to cut loose and march South to the Ocean. We are in fine shape and I think could go anywhere Uncle Billy [General Sherman] would lead.

On Friday, November 11, the last train was leaving Atlanta, bound for Chattanooga. It was filled with evacuees from the city. "We are obliged to stay here now," observed Carrie Berry after seeing her Aunt Marthy off to the car shed. The few remaining residents grew anxious. Carrie wrote with growing alarm:

Nov. 12. *We were fritened almost to death last night. Some mean soldiers set several houses on fire in different parts of the town. I could not go to sleep for fear that they would set our house on fire. We all dred the next few days to come for they said that they would set the last house on fire if they had to leave this place.*

Nov. 13. *The federal soldiers have been coming to day and burning houses and I have ben looking at them come in nearly all day.*

Nov. 14. *They came burning Atlanta to day. We all dread it because they say they will burn the last house before they stop. We will dread it.*

Nov. 15. *This has been a dreadful day. Things have been burning all around us. We dread to night because we do not know what moment they will set our house on fire.*

That same night, drummer boy William Bircher from Minnesota wrote in his diary:

> *At night we destroyed the city by fire. A grand and awful spectacle it presented to the beholder. . . . The heaven was one expanse of lurid fire; the air was filled with flying, burning cinders. Buildings, covering two hundred acres, were in ruins or in flames; every instant there was the sharp detonation of the smothered, booming sound of exploding shells and powder concealed in the buildings, and then the sparks and flames would shoot up into the black and red roof, scattering cinders far and wide. . . . I heard the real fine band of the Thirty-third Massachusetts playing, "John Brown's soul goes marching on," by the light of the burning buildings.*

Observed Theodore Upson: "We have utterly destroyed Atlanta. I don't think any people will want to try and live there now. It is pretty tough to rout people out of their homes in this way, but it is war."

Surrounded by the ruins of her city, Carrie Berry reported what it was like to have lived through the inferno of a man-made firestorm. She wrote on November 16:

> *Oh what a night we had. They came burning the store house and about night it looked like the whole town was on fire. We all set up all night. If we had not sat up our house would have been burnt up for the fire was very near and the soldiers were going around setting houses on fire where they were not watched. They behaved very badly. They all left town about one o'clock this evening and we were glad when they left for no body knows what we have suffered since they came in.*

The ruined city was still home for about fifty families who had remained in Atlanta until the very end. When General Sherman rode out of town on the morning of November 16, 1864, the boy Noble Williams and two of his friends tramped all the way to the outskirts of the city. He never forgot the awesome view he encountered on that day:

> *The country for miles around presented a scene of almost unequalled desolation. Many trees had fallen . . . and those left standing were but a shattered remnants of their former selves. . . . The woods and fields were strewn with carcasses of dead and decaying animals most of which . . . becoming disabled, were shot or left to die of starvation.*

Carrie Berry stayed close to her home and watched as hordes of Confederate scavengers—both soldiers and civilians—invaded her city. Men, women, and children—black and white—picked whatever they considered valuable from the smoking buildings and rubble. Many had come from the countryside. They loaded coffee, sugar, bacon, salt, iron, and hides onto their carts and wagons, eager to get as much loot as they could carry.

"We have been picking up some things," Carrie wrote on November 17. And on November 18: "We children have been plundering about to-day seeing what we could find."

Four days after the burning of her city, Carrie Berry and her mother managed to return to the domestic chores that kept them busy and, no doubt, preserved their sanity. "Mama and me have been ironing to-day," she wrote on November 19. "We have begun to feel at home but it doesn't look like Atlanta. The citizens all met at the City Hall. There are [only] eighty men in town."

It was cold and snowing outside. Carrie was grateful that she and her parents still had their little house and could warm themselves by a fire. Food supplies were scarce. Carrie and her girlfriend went to collect hickory nuts that were distributed at city hall and patiently, for days on end, picked up iron nails in the rubble of their neighborhood to use for barter.

By the end of November, the girl's diary entries were more cheerful. "This has been a beautiful day," she wrote on a sunny Sunday afternoon. "There have been a grate many citizens coming back. . . . It won't be very long untill they get the railroad fixed up from here to Macon and then I hope I can see Grandma." A week later Carrie's mother delivered a healthy baby girl. "I had a little sister this morning at eight o'clock," Carrie wrote on December 7. "Mama gave her to me. I think it's very pretty." Life went on amidst the rubble, and Carrie had now a new reason to rejoice.

Throughout a cold December, Carrie Berry kept busy. "I have been cooking and cleaning house and waiting on Mama and [baby] sister Maggy," is a constant refrain in her diary. Amidst the account of all her chores, there was also the anticipation of her favorite holiday. "Every moment I can get I am making things to do on the tree," is a theme that echoes through the weeks to come. In the darkest days of a dark year, Carrie Berry would write:

Dec. 20. *I have been buisy making presents all day. I went down to Mrs. Lesters [her neighbor] to make Mamas. . . . I think it is so pretty. I fear we will not get through with our presents. Christmas is getting so near.*

Dec. 22. *We went to get our Christmas tree this evening. It was very cold but we did not feel it we were so excited about it.*

Dec. 24. *I have been buisy to day making cakes to trim the tree. . . . I have it all ready trimed and we are all going to night to see it. I think it looks very pretty. We will be sorry when it is all over.*

Dec. 25. We all went down to-night to see the tree and how pretty it looked. The room was full of ladies and children and Cap. gave us music on the piano and tried all he could to make us enjoy our selves and we did have a merry time.

The next day her father left for Macon to be tried in a Confederate court for staying in Atlanta with the Yankees. "We are afraid they will put him in the Army," confided his daughter to her diary. "We all feel very sad."

Her fears were unfounded. Her father rejoined his family within a fortnight. On January 2, 1865, Carrie and her friends went back to school. "Ella, me and Buddie are studying arithmetic, spelling, reading and geography," she noted in her diary. "We are all trying to see which will learn the most. . . . We have to study very hard and we don't get time to do much of anything but we have been playing long enough to spend time on our books."

Two months after the dreadful fire, Carrie Berry attended the first church service in the city since the siege and the shelling and the endless suffering had begun in August 1864. She wrote on Sunday, January 15, 1865: "We are all so glad that we could have church once more this evening and went out to the cemetery."

The next day she noted—with childish pride—"We started to school irly this morning and had perfect lessons all day. I missed [only] one wird and that was in spelling."

— 9 —

THE ABOMINATION
OF DESOLATION

THE DAY AFTER THE BURNING OF ATLANTA, Theodore Upson wrote to his parents back in Indiana:

We are marching South. . . . Such an Army as we have I doubt if ever was got together before; all are in the finest condition. We have weeded out all the sick, feeble ones and all the faint hearted ones and all the boys are ready for a meal or a fight and don't seem to care which it is. We have learned to get along with little in the way of baggage too. All a good many carry is a blanket made into a roll with their rubber "poncho" which is doubled around and tied at the ends and hung over the left shoulder. Of course we have our haversacks and canteens and our guns and cartridge boxes with 40 rounds of ammunition. Some of the boys carry 20 more in their pockets.

Many of the soldiers who marched with General Sherman through Georgia and the Carolinas were boys under eighteen, too young to vote in the recent election that had kept Abraham Lincoln in the White House. "My little devils," Sherman called them, and they would think of him fondly as "Uncle Billy." One of them, Cordy Foote, age fifteen, a drummer boy from Michigan, remembered when he met the general on the eve of the second day of the march. It had rained continuously, and he and his companions were cold and wet. They poked about, in vain, trying to nurse a fire for bacon and coffee from a log of wet wood.

"Try a poncho over it, boys," said a soldier wearing an overcoat with a cape and a slouch hat drawn down over his eyes, who had been watching them. They did, and at last a spark was roused, and then a few flames began to flicker. "There you have it," said the soldier. "Thank you, Uncle

Billy," replied Cord, as he grinned up into the red-bearded face of the stranger. Even as an old man, Cordy Foote would remember General Sherman's smile as he nodded and walked away.

William Bircher, the drummer boy from Minnesota, observed the foraging during the first week of the march:

> *Each brigade organized a . . . foraging party—we called them "Bummers"—under the command of one or more discreet officers, who gathered near the route traveled corn or forage of any kind, meat of all kinds, vegetables, cornmeal, or whatever was needed by the command. . . . Their aim was at all times to keep in the wagon trains at least ten day's rations. . . . Soldiers were ordered not to enter the dwellings of the inhabitants or to commit any trespass.*

These orders were soon disregarded. Dolly Sumner Burge, a young widow who was a native of Maine and a relative of the abolitionist leader Charles Sumner, was among thousands of lone women with young children to plead for Federal guards to protect her property.

Dolly was visited by soldiers from Sherman's army on her cotton plantation near Covington, Georgia, three days after the march to the sea had begun. She was alone but for her nine-year-old daughter and her slaves. A sympathetic Union officer had provided her with a guard, but she soon learned that nothing could halt the swarming looters that broke into her smokehouse, dairy, pantry, kitchen, and cellar. "Like famished wolves they came, breaking locks and whatever is in the way," she wrote in her diary on November 19, 1864.

The rear guard arrived the next morning, mild-mannered soldiers who only asked for a bucket of water for boiling coffee. "Thus ended the passing of Sherman's army by my place," mourned Dolly, "leaving me poorer by $38,000 than I was yesterday. . . . And a much stronger Rebel. . . ."

Fifteen-year-old Cordy Foote soon got caught up in an impromptu foraging expedition of his own. Finding no pork or poultry, he and his friends looked for buried treasure in the lawn surrounding an old plantation. They unearthed a chest of finery and family heirlooms. Cord dressed himself in an evening gown and paraded in silks and laces in front of the colonnaded porch where the young ladies of the family watched helplessly as soldiers carried their loot away. When the foragers returned to camp that night, they dressed up in satins and velvets confiscated from the family chests. The camp looked like a fancy dress ball, but young Cord was uneasy. Lying on his cot, staring into the dark, he wondered why war made a fellow do things against his own nature. He would remember that incident as an old man, still ashamed of what he had done that afternoon.

At the end of the first week of Sherman's march to the sea, Theodore Upson's brigade ran into serious opposition. At Griswoldville, Georgia, a pick-up force of boys and old men hurled themselves against his Indiana regiment. In desperation, the Confederates had cleaned the Georgia countryside of every male who could carry a gun and herded them into battle. They were wiped out. Theodore Upson remembered:

We went down on the line where lay the dead of the Confederates. It was a terrible sight. Some one was groaning. We moved a few bodies, and there was a boy with a broken arm and leg—just a boy 14 years old; and beside him, cold in death, lay his father, two brothers, and an uncle. It was a harvest of death. We brought the poor fellow up to the fire. Our surgeons made him as comfortable as they could. Then we marched away leaving him with his own wounded who we could no longer care for.

One of Upson's officers found a young boy looking up steadily at the bluecoats. "Water," he said, "can you give me some water?" His chest was torn, the breastbone protruding. The Union soldiers saw the beating of the exposed heart. "We never wanted to fight," the youth said. "The cavalry rounded us up and drove us in and made us march."

The Confederate resistance was futile. On November 23, 1864, William Bircher's Minnesota brigade entered Milledgeville, the capital of Georgia, where the state legislature had hurriedly absconded on hearing of Sherman's approach. The drummer boy observed the panic that had spread to the citizens, the overcrowded trains and overflowing vehicles that carried the fugitives out of town. "Only a few of us entered the city," he wrote in his diary. "The magazines, arsenals, depots, factories and storehouses containing property belonging to the Confederate government were burned, also some seventeen hundred bales of cotton. Private dwellings were respected, and no instance occurred of pillage or of insult to the people." Some of the Federal soldiers boiled their coffee over bonfires of Confederate currency and held a mock session of the legislature that passed a resolution to rejoin the Union.

Despite the efforts of Sherman's officers, thousands of slaves had fallen behind the line of the march. Theodore Upson's regiment was followed by "vast numbers" of black women with babies in their arms or clinging to their skirts who plodded mile after mile, determined to escape to freedom. An officer of his company saw two little boys, four or five years old, hidden in a wagon by a weary woman too exhausted to continue on her own, "intending that they should see the land of freedom if she couldn't." Some babies, perched upon the backs of mules, tumbled off and were abandoned by the roadside or drowned in swamps and streams.

Southern refugee family taking to the road (courtesy of the Library of Congress)

At one of the river crossings a large black woman embraced Cord Foote, the drummer boy from Michigan. "We'un done heered dis wuz an army ob debils fum hell, but praise de Lawd, praise de Lawd," she sobbed, "it's de Lawd's own babes an' sucklin's!" Cord extracted himself from her embrace with all the dignity of his fifteen years while his fellow soldiers roared with laughter.

During the second week of the march, Sherman's soldiers grew weary. Wrote William Bircher on November 25, after crossing the Oconee River:

We lost poor Henry Simmers, the drummer of Company G during the night. The poor fellow, being unable to keep up, lay down somewhere along the road, and was captured by the cavalry that was following us. I took his blanket and drum to relieve him, but he was too fatigued to follow, saying, "Oh, let me rest. Let me sleep a short time. Then I will follow on." I tried to keep him under my eye, but he finally eluded me, and when we again stopped for a short rest he was not to be found. . . . I pitied the poor fellow. I was afraid he would never live to return home.

Bircher's fears were justified. That same week, to the army's rear, a seventeen-year-old Union soldier was being buried—a homesick boy from Iowa who had escaped from his camp one night, but was captured a few miles away and put on trial for treason. His court martial was unmoved by his pathetic defense: "I just wanted to see my mother." The boy was shot by a firing squad and buried beside the Oconee River.

Two of Sherman's columns, the Fourteenth and Twentieth Corps, were marching along roads that brought them together at Sandersville, some twenty-five miles southeast of Georgia's capital. Living with her mother-in-law in that town was a seventeen-year-old war widow with an infant son, known in her memoirs only by the initials L.F.J. She wrote of her encounter with the Union troops.

> *I ventured to a front window that faced the two roads leading to the capital. . . . Looking out I screamed in horror [at] the rush of Yankee ruffians. . . . All day long the men and wagons poured into town. . . . No yards, no gardens were spared in our ill-fated village. . . . The soldiers . . . would walk up the steps of the back veranda on which we stood, and throwing down the hams and shoulders of our meat, would cut them up . . . in our very faces.*
>
> *Next they found the sugar, flour, lard, salt, syrup which mother had stored away in a cellar dug beneath one of the Negro houses. . . . Like statues mother and I stood looking on, and saw them take all the provisions we had, then kill the milk cow and other stock about the lot—saw them find the wheat and grain we had hidden in the attic behind the wall; stood silent and sad as we saw the "potato hill" robbed, and knew that now our last hope for food was gone. . . . That night we went to bed supperless. . . . Sadly I had seen the rice, sugar, coffee, and lard taken from the storerooms . . . but sadder now was the thought, "The cows are killed. I will be so hungry I cannot nurse Baby."*

The desperate mother had unexpected help from a young Union soldier who had been placed as a guard on her premises on the second day of the occupation. When he heard her baby's low wail and learned she was unable to nurse him, he offered to share the rations he would draw in the evening. True to his word, he brought her flour and coffee. "At sundown," wrote L.F.J., "a Boy in Blue supped with the widow of a Boy in Gray right in the midst of the enemy's land surrounded by the Federal army!"

Elsewhere, other Union soldiers showed their compassion for the victims of the war. Not far from Sandersville, a foraging party from a Michigan regiment found two small girls, about three and five years old, in a remote log cabin. Their faces and bodies were caked with mud, and they wore thin cotton dresses, made from sacks, with holes ripped out for arms.

The troops found no trace of their parents. The soldiers built a fire, bathed the girls and washed and combed their hair. They stole clothing for the little girls and dressed them in the best the countryside could afford. The girls rode a pack mule all day, and when the "bummers" camped at night, each slept in a soldier's arm. The children were turned over to the regiment the following night and began their long ride to Savannah [and an adopted home] on the back of Union soldiers who cared for them as if they were their own daughters.

Slashed roads and desultory fighting halted the progress of Sherman's army in the last days of November. They now began to burn houses and barns along the way. Jennie Pye was just a little girl when Federal troops came to her home that November. She remembered vividly:

When Sherman's raiders came to our house they demanded of my mother all the money and valuables she had and told her they would give her fifteen minutes to clear the house as they would burn it and take the things they wanted; however, they did not burn the house, but burned the gin house instead where there was lots of cotton. My mother . . . [put] all the silver and jewelry she had in a deep box and put it under her hen nest where she had a hen sitting. . . . Then they dragged grandma Nelson all around the house, trying to make her tell where the men and stock were, but she refused to reveal their hiding places.

Day after day, Cord Foote saw as if it were for the first time the grief and terror of utterly helpless women and children, and it made him feel sick at heart. So did the dreadful tales of the shadowlike men with hunted eyes who crept into his camp at night. Gaunt and emaciated, they told of the horrors of the Andersonville prison where many thousands of Union soldiers had died from disease and starvation. "They's thousands of us fellows still there," said a soldier who looked more dead than alive.

The march grew more and more difficult during the first weeks of December. Foragers were now frequently harried by Confederate cavalrymen who took cover in the pine woods surrounding swampy waters. Sherman's men had to clear slashed roads every day. As they neared the coast, many sluggish creeks slowed their progress, and swampy waters often concealed treacherous quicksand. The soldiers now had to rely mostly on rationed bacon and hardtack brought from Atlanta in covered wagons. On Sunday, December 10, William Bircher went on a little foraging expedition of his own to supplement his meager rations:

I . . . came to a very fine plantation, where the white folks had all run off, leaving nobody at home, but an old negro couple. I was the first Union soldier they had seen. After I told them that they were now free and could go where they wished, and that I was one of "Massa Lincum's" soldiers, their joy knew no bounds. Nothing was too good for me. . . . The old darky proceeded to the garden and dug about a peck of yams, and the old lady went to the barn and got me about two dozen eggs. She also gave me a piece of bacon.

Four days later, on December 14, Sherman's Fifteenth Corps captured Fort McAllister, near the mouth of the Ogeechee River. In two more days there was open communication with the sea. The mail brought by the Union fleet from the North was eagerly welcomed, for the men had neither received nor sent any letters in nearly six weeks. Wrote the teenager George Drake to his parents in Illinois on December 17:

> *I sit down this evening to write a few lines for the first time in a long time. . . . We have been cut off from communication for some time, but . . . mail came in to-day. I got 4 letters. We have had a hard trip. . . . I saw a good deal I would like to tell you about. Maybe if I live I can tell it to you. I can tell you one thing without stretching it a bit. I marched seventeen days without a bit of bread but I lived on fresh pork and sweet potatoes.*
>
> *We were surrounded by the rebbel cavalry all the time. . . . Some of our boys in our regiment was taken and the rebbels put them on horseback and started them to the rear. Their officers told them that they had better put them out of the way. . . . They shot a sargent in our regiment 2 times in the head. So he fell off his horse on the ground on his face and made believe dead . . . they went off and left him. Afterward some of the boys fetched him in camp.*

Meanwhile, Sherman's own cavalry was prowling several miles to the siege line that enclosed the city of Savannah. On its southern flank, the horsemen began to prey on the rich farmlands of Liberty County. The small boys in that county had suddenly disappeared. Women on the plantations were terrified by rumors that the Yankees would kill all male children. At the first sighting of bluecoated Union soldiers, mothers would disguise their sons in girl's clothing. In one farmhouse, Sherman's raiders admired a pretty child in a freshly starched dress who slid down the stair rail at breakneck speed. His distraught mother called out: "Bessie, my son, come down from there." The troopers burst into laughter and left without harming mother or child.

By the beginning of the third week of December, the last Georgia militiamen began to retreat from their positions. Among them was Leroy West Harris, age sixteen, one of the few Griswoldville survivors. He was barefoot. Patriotic ladies in Savannah had sent a wagon-load of high-heeled women's shoes to the Confederate troops. Harris had been given a pair "only large enough for my sixteen-year-old toes to stick in" and had thrown them away.

As his command struggled through Savannah, the hungry boy entered a grocery store and gazed at a showcase filled with yams. "Oh, if I had just one of them," he said. The owner, a formidable looking Irish woman, surrendered: "God bless your heart, you shall have one. You ought to be at home with your mammy." Leroy left town with the sweet potato cradled inside his shirt. *His* war ended on December 21, when the Confederates evacuated Savannah.

The next day, December 22, 1864, Sherman sent Lincoln a telegram: "I beg to present you, as a Christmas gift, the city of Savannah, with 150 heavy guns and plenty of ammunition, also about 25,000 bales of cotton."

Since they had begun their march from Atlanta in mid-November, Sherman's troops had crossed four hundred twenty-five miles of hostile territory and done some one hundred million dollars worth of damage.

> *Darkest of all Decembers*
> *Ever my life has known,*
> *Sitting here by the embers*
> *Stunned- helpless- alone.*

wrote Mary Chesnut in her diary when she heard the news of Savannah's fall.

The week before Christmas, the teenager Eliza Andrews traveled over a broken railroad system and in wagons from Washington, Georgia, to a plantation near Albany, across the route of Sherman's march. On Christmas Eve, December 24, 1864, she wrote in her "wartime journal":

> *We struck the "burnt country" as it is well named by the natives, and then I could better understand the wrath and desperation of these poor people. I almost felt as if I should like to hang a Yankee myself. There was hardly a fence left standing from Sparta to Gordon. The fields were trampled down and the road was lined with carcasses of horses, hogs and cattle, that the invaders, unable either to consume or carry away with them, had wantonly shot down to starve out the people and prevent them from making their crops. The stench in some places was unbearable.... The dwellings that were standing all showed signs of pillage and on every plantation we saw the charred remains of the ginhouses.... Crowds of [Confederate] soldiers were tramping over the road in both direction[s].... They were mostly on foot, and I saw numbers seated on the roadside greedily eating raw turnips, meat skins, parched corn—anything they could find, even picking up the loose grain that Sherman's horses had left.*

Savannah, by comparison, had remained an oasis of beauty and tranquillity. The day before Christmas, William Bircher went into the city and marveled at the wide streets, the beautiful parks, the architecture of the churches and public buildings, and the "very fine and tasty buildings" in the residential areas. "Everything in the city indicated wealth and refinement," he noted in his diary. In stark contrast he spent Christmas Eve with his comrades in camp with no protection but their tents pitched on the hard frozen ground. He wrote:

> *It was hard to be homeless at this merry season when folks up North were having such happy times. But it was wonderful how elastic the spirits of our soldiers were, and how jolly they could be under the most adverse cir-cumstances. . . . We began to drop off to sleep, some rolling themselves up in their blankets and overcoats and lying down, Indian fashion, feet to the fire, while others crept off to their cold shelter tents under the snow-laden pine trees for what poor rest they could find . . . wishing each other a "Merry Christmas."*

Theodore Upson had a better time on Christmas Day. He wrote to his parents:

> *We have been having a Christmas Jubilee. The boys raised some money and I went down into the City to get some stuff. We have a Darky cook, and he said "You alls get the greginces [ingredients] and I will get you alls up a fine dinner sure." I got some chickens, canned goods, condensed milk and a dozen eggs. . . . Some of the officers had a banquet—[so] they called it. I don't know if they had egg nog. If they did, their eggs must have been better than ours, but I know they must have had some sort of nog for the Provost Guard had to help some of them to their Quarters.*

Cordy Foote spent the day after Christmas polishing brass buttons and the silver mountings of his drum. On December 27 was the grand review by General Sherman in Savannah. The day was clear and sunny. Cord marched at the head of his Michigan regiment one pace behind the color-bearer.

With bands playing and drums rolling, Sherman's men marched down the wide oak-lined streets of Savannah, marveling at the magnificent mansions that stood behind iron fences. That night in camp, Cordy had his first taste of oysters—and his last taste of shared comradeship with his friends in his company. The end of Cord's three-year enlistment was at hand, and he was filled with sadness.

General Sherman, too, was grieving. His elation over the capture of Sa-vannah had been marred by a private tragedy. He learned of the death of his six-month-old son Charles, whom he had never seen, from a news-paper brought into the city. He wrote to his wife of the baby's death: "All spoke of him as so bright and fair that I had hoped he would be spared us to fill the great void left in our hearts by Willy [another son, who had died from typhoid fever]. But it is otherwise decreed and we must submit."

The general found some solace among the people of Savannah—especially in the company of two little girls, Nelly and Daisy Gordon, whose uncle was a Federal colonel and one of the general's oldest friends. When he brought letters to their mother a few days after the parade, Mrs. Gordon drew her daughter Nelly forth and said: "General, here is a little girl who was very anxious to see 'old Sherman' the day of the parade." Nelly's voice trembled: "I never said 'old Sherman'—it was Daisy!" "Well, you said it, too, Nelly," Daisy snapped. "You did say 'old Sherman'!"

To their surprise, the general took the girls on his knees and began teasing them: "Why of course you never said 'old Sherman,' because you and I used to play together when I was a little boy, and now we are going to sit right down and talk it over." The Union general and the daughters of a Confederate cavalry officer became fast friends.

But Sherman was well aware of his reputation as a vandal who made war on helpless civilians. To his daughter Minnie, who was in school in Notre Dame, Indiana, he wrote:

> *Think of how cruel men become in war, when even your Papa has to do such acts. Pray every night that the war may end. Hundreds of children like yourself are daily taught to curse my name, and every night thousands kneel in prayer and beseech the Almighty to consign me to perdition.*

William Bircher's Minnesota regiment remained in camp for the first two weeks of January 1865, drilling and doing camp and police duty. Every other day he visited Savannah. One evening as he and a few of his companions were returning from the theater, they passed a fine residence where some ladies in the second-story window were singing "Bonny Blue Flag" and "Maryland, My Maryland!" He wrote in his diary:

> *We stopped and listened a few moments. When they got through, we commenced and sung that grand old anthem "The Star Spangled Banner." I don't think there ever was such a surprise in that house before. I don't think "The Star Spangled Banner" ever sounded grander or sweeter than it did that night in the still, dark streets of Savannah, sung by the boys in blue. They raised the window and requested us to sing "Red, White, and Blue," and the ladies accompanied us. They thanked us, bid us good night, and invited us to come down some evening and repeat the programme.*

There was no time for a repeat performance. General Sherman was about to turn his columns northward into the Carolinas. Wrote William Bircher on February 5: "We marched with unfurled flags, men cheering, and singing . . . crossing the Savannah River into South Carolina. Our army did not lack enthusiasm." Sherman's men would be still harsher in

South Carolina than they had been in Georgia. "If there is any place they ought to fight and fight hard it is right here where treason first was hatched," wrote Theodore Upson.

In Columbia, the capital of South Carolina, where the bells of secession had first rung out, young Emma LeConte, daughter of a chemistry professor, wrote in her "wartime diary":

How dreadfully sick I am of this war. . . . It commenced when I was thirteen, and I am now seventeen and no prospect yet of its ending. No pleasure, no enjoyment—nothing . . . but the stern realities of life. We have only the saddest anticipations and the dread of hardships and cares, when bright dreams of the future ought to shine on us.

Among the Yankees approaching her town was William Bircher. On February 8 he wrote: "The whole army was burning with the insatiable desire to wreck vengeance on South Carolina. I almost trembled at her fate but felt that she deserved all that seemed in store for her."

Six days later, on February 14, Emma LeConte jotted in her diary: "What a panic the whole town is in! . . . The Yankees are reported a few miles off [Columbia] on the other side of the river. . . . I do not feel half as frightened as I thought I would."

Hastily, government transportation was requisitioned. Train after train, filled with supplies, left Columbia, and anxious families waited for hours at the passenger depot hoping to secure a seat. William Bircher's regiment was approaching Columbia. On February 15 he wrote: "The fences and buildings, the entire length of our day's march, were burning, and the smoke nearly suffocated us."

That same day Theodore Upson wrote to his parents in Indiana:

We are nearing the city of Columbia, S.C. Last night as we were marching up the valley some one began to sing "John Brown's body lies a smoldering in the grave but his soul is marching on." It was grand! The words of the song sung by perhaps 30,000 seasoned veterans rolled up and down the valley. I think the Johnnys must have heard it for they are just across the River. . . . Our boys are getting to have an utter contempt of them.

The next day, February 16, Sherman's troops began shelling the city, and preparations for an immediate evacuation of Columbia were completed. That night the governor and a train of state officials left town. Some remnants of the Confederate cavalry remained in the city until the morning of February 17. By then, the population of Columbia had dwindled to about twenty thousand, the majority being white women and children and black servants. General Sherman entered Columbia about two o'clock in the afternoon of February 17 and promised the mayor full protection of the city.

During the shelling of Columbia, Emma LeConte, her mother, and her sister Sally had moved into the back basement room of their home on the campus of South Carolina College. In the afternoon on February 17, she heard the shouting of the Union troops.

> *I ran to . . . my bedroom windows just in time to see the U.S. flag run up over the State House. Oh, what a horrid sight! What degradation! After four long bitter years of bloodshed and hatred, now to float there at last! That hateful symbol of despotism! I do not think I could possibly describe my feeling. I know I could not look at it.*

Worse was to come. The next day, in the evening, Columbia was set ablaze. Sherman blamed retreating Confederates; Southerners, like Emma LeConte, accused drunken Union men. She wrote: "This is civilized warfare. This is the way the 'cultured' Yankee nation wars upon women and children! Failing with our men in the field, *this* is the way they must conquer! It is so easy to burn the homes over the heads of helpless women and children, and turn them with insults and sneers into the streets."

Theodore Upson's regiment was ordered into the city that night. In a letter to his parents in Indiana he gave a different account of the behavior of the Union troops who came to the rescue:

> *Rows of cotton bales were burning fiercely, so were some of the buildings along the street. A good many of our men were drunk. Our first business was to gather them up and get them out of the way. . . . The wind blew terribly. It would pick up flakes of the burning cotton. . . . If it fell on a roof it set fire to that building. . . . We soon began to help the women and children. Poor souls! All we could do was to hustle them out and, if they had any valuables, help them get them to a safe place. Many of them were in their night clothes. . . . Where we could get blankets we gave them away. . . . Some of the women we had to carry . . . and the little children, too. Our men . . . were kind and careful. . . . I don't believe there was a man among them who had any thought except to do all in his power for those helpless stricken people. . . . We were not fighting women and children.*

Fifteen-year-old Mary Janney, daughter of the proprietor of a downtown hotel, saw her house collapsing during the fire. She was moved by the compassion of a Yankee soldier who, like her father, was a Quaker and opposed to war. At great risk to his own life, he saved Mary's trunk and piano from the burning rubble and saw to it that his provisions were shared among the homeless family.

Mary and her parents spent the night at the Fifteenth Army encampment as the guests of a colonel from Illinois. She remembered: "They treated us well. They offered us wine, coffee and crackers; but I wouldn't touch a thing; father and mother gladly accepted the coffee. We stayed there until some time in the morning."

A little more than a mile away from the Janneys' hotel, schoolgirls from the Ursuline convent were kneeling in front of the altar, reciting the rosary, trying to keep up their courage. One of them, Sara Aldrich, remembered:

How many hours we remained on our knees . . . I can't tell. But I do remember how we were suddenly brought to our feet by the awful cry, "The convent is on fire. . . . Good Father Lawrence collected us in the lower hall . . . to march us in some order to the Catholic Church, at that time beyond the falling houses and the fierce flames. We marched through the blazing streets with the precision of a military band. . . . Not a cry, not a moan. The roaring of the fires, the scorching flames on either side . . . did not create the least disorder. [Never will I forget] that majestic figure of the Mother Superior in the graceful habit of the Ursuline . . . the long line of anxious, white young faces of the schoolgirls.

It was almost dawn on February 18 when the nuns led the girls into the church. The sisters calmed the sobbing children and watched over them until they fell asleep on the cushioned pews. A short time later, the door burst open and drunken soldiers shouted, "All out! We are blowing up the church!" The girls fled in terror to the churchyard, hiding behind hedges and tombstones. Officers soon arrived and drove off the drunken men.

The children refused to reenter the church. They huddled by the doorway until sunrise. They were there, grouped around the Mother Superior, when Sherman arrived. His daughter, Minnie, had once been a pupil of the Ursuline nun, and Sister Baptista Lynn was not intimidated by the general. She stood, remembered Sara Aldrich, "erect and proudly, with the air of an injured empress dethroned" and accepted the general's apologies.

Sherman's men stayed in Columbia only a few days. On February 20, Emma LeConte noted in her diary: "Shortly after breakfast—oh, joyful sight—the two corps encamped behind the Campus back of us marched by with their immense wagon trains. They tell us all will be gone by tomorrow evening." The next day, she ventured forth into the center of town.

Yes, I have seen it all—I have seen the 'Abomination of Desolation.' It is even worse than I thought. The place is literally in ruins. The entire heart of the city is ashes. Standing in the center of town, as far as the eye can reach, nothing to be seen but heaps of rubbish, tall dreary chimneys and shattered brick walls. . . . Poor old Columbia—where is all her beauty so admired by strangers, so loved by her children! The wind moans among the black chimneys and whistles through the gaping windows. . . . I reached home sad at heart.

Her diary entry a week later reveals the girl's resiliency:

I am now fairly launched as a schoolma'am. I fancy I get on pretty well considering my lack of experience. I teach [sister] Sally arithmetic, Latin, spelling and elementary natural philosophy besides reading and composition. I will begin [the] study [of French and German] myself. . . . At the marketplace yesterday we saw the old bell—"secessia"—that had rung out every state as it seceded, lying half-buried in the earth and reminding me . . . "that all things earthly disappear."

Sherman's soldiers, meanwhile, marched on to Winnsboro, South Carolina, and then to Fayetteville, North Carolina. Before leaving Winnsboro, Sherman's army destroyed about thirty buildings, including the Episcopal church. An anonymous young girl whose father was the postmaster of the town related the story of their two-day occupation:

The streets and vacant lots were filled with homeless families, many . . . having nothing but the clothes they wore; when bringing bedding, raiment or provisions out of their burning homes, these were destroyed by the brutal soldiers. They stole much that was useless to them, for even Bibles were taken. . . . The yards and gardens were perforated with bayonets, men searching for buried treasure.

The army left no food in town. "We were very short of rations," noted the drummer boy William Bircher. For nearly three weeks his Minnesota regiment marched north, heading for the North Carolina border. It rained continuously, and they were stuck in the mud all along the road. On March 2 he wrote:

Rained all day. We marched twenty miles. The roads were in a horrible condition. We lay in the woods all night in our wet clothes, as it rained all night. We had but the clothes on our backs, and of course could not change, so matters were mighty uncomfortable. Daylight of the 3rd . . . brought us no comfort. . . . With a cup of coffee and a few black peas we continued.

A week later the weather turned fair and clear. Bircher's regiment had crossed the state line into North Carolina and reached Fayetteville on March 11, "where we found an abundance of flour, bacon, molasses, coffee and tobacco, and lived on the best the country afforded." During their

Ruins of Charleston, South Carolina (courtesy of the Library of Congress)

stay in town they were ordered to destroy the arsenal and a large cotton mill. "The poor people in the neighborhood, who had always worked there, begged to have it saved, as it was their only means of support," Bircher wrote on March 15.

Sally Hawthorne was the young daughter of the owner of the largest cotton mill in Fayetteville. She remembered the Yankee occupation and the pain the destruction of the mill brought to her father and to the families who worked for him. On the morning of the arrival of Sherman's troops, she and her little sisters stood on the main street of their hometown, handing out sandwiches to the fleeing Confederate soldiers.

> *I will never forget that scene. A wide street filled with Confederate soldiers on horseback, riding pell mell up the street, on the sidewalk, anywhere, so as to be going uptown. As they passed by near enough to reach the sandwiches, they would bend for the packages, and then go on at breakneck speed. We . . . held the basket up close to the passing men till nearly all were gone . . . when there came a great noise of guns, big ones, too.*

General Oliver Howard's division swiftly appropriated her house, barns, and stable. For five days, Sally, her mother who "refused to leave her room," her father, and a houseful of young brothers and sisters were under strict orders from the invaders. Her twelve-year-old brother barely escaped being shot by one of the guards. He was dressed in gray, cut-down from his brother's old uniform, and had an old cavalry cap on his head; hence the guard mistook him for an escaped Confederate.

Her family was kindly treated, but Sally's father was soon notified that his cotton factory [where much of his money was invested] would be blown up. The mayor and the town board asked for an audience with General Sherman and pleaded with him to keep the buildings and machinery intact for the sake of the operatives, all of them originally from the North, who knew nothing but spinning and weaving. There was nothing else these men and women could do for a livelihood.

General Sherman listened to their argument but did not rescind his order. Sally's father, accompanied by a guard, notified all the mill hands himself, urging them to take all the cotton and thread and rolls of sheeting they wanted. Exactly at three o'clock on March 15, the mill went up with a terrible noise, and dense smoke surrounded the town for hours.

The next day, Sherman's troops departed. All that afternoon could be heard the rumble of the army moving and the tread of the cavalry. Left on main street were looted stores and dead horses. "That is the most gruesome sound," Sally remembered, "the scream of a mortally wounded horse." Nothing seemed to slow Sherman's soldiers.

The back roads of the South were filled with refugees—women searching for their babies . . . others sitting in the dust and crying. Thousands fled all the way to Texas; thousands more streamed toward Richmond, hoping the Confederate government might provide a safe home for them. It was too late—Jeff Davis had no food or shelter to give. The Confederacy was dying.

— 10 —

THE NIGHTMARE
IS OVER

N EAR MOUNT JACKSON, VIRGINIA, seven-year-old Robert Hugh
Martin witnessed from the front porch of his home some of the last war
scenes in his part of the country. He had been let out of school because
"the Yankees were coming." On March 2, 1865, General Philip H. Sheridan attacked and scattered the "threads and patches" of what was once
General Early's proud army.

The boy watched nearly all day long as columns of Confederate and
Union cavalry skirmished along the hills that border the Shenandoah
River—until the Confederates returned no more.

On March 6 and 7, Union troops came through his town with their
Confederate prisoners: First, a solid mass of cavalry in blue to clear the
way, and then a column of gray on foot, with soldiers in blue riding on
the sidelines as guards. Robert remembered:

*As soon as my folks could discern the column of gray . . . they brought out
some rather large baskets containing what looked to me like soda or water
crackers. I begged for some, only to be denied. I followed the baskets as they
were carried to the front upper porch when, looking around, I saw that
every house or yard had its womenfolk with similar baskets and all lined up
as near the street as they could get. As the men in gray trudged by, the
women began to toss the food into the ranks. The men seemed ravenously
hungry and there was a mad scramble to catch a flying piece of cracker.*

As an old man, Robert could still picture the distressed look of the men
in the middle of the prisoners' column who saw crackers falling all
around them but had to trudge on foodless. "Child as I was," he would

write, "I was sure the end was near. . . . I wanted the war over *at once* . . . to stop all this killing and wounding and the long series of privations ever getting worse . . . the ever shorter rations of food that I could hardly eat. I [had] wearied of the salt pork and the cornbread made without milk, the rye coffee sweetened with sorghum molasses. . . . All these were too heavy for my stomach and I *did* nearly starve."

Conditions in Richmond were equally distressing: A single stick of firewood cost five dollars now, a barrel of flour $425. During the nine months siege of nearby Petersburg, General Grant's troops had slowly but steadily extended their trenches, threatening the thinning Confederate lines to the capital of the Confederacy.

Those who could left Richmond in the waning days of March, seeking safety further south. Among the departing civilians was seventeen-year-old Louise Wigfall, daughter of a Confederate senator from Texas, and her younger sister. She wrote of their departure, "It was a lovely evening late in March. . . . As the train pulled out and ran slowly across the long bridge over the James, we watched with aching hearts the sunshine lingering with loving light on the towers and spires of the city."

Guns boomed all day east of Richmond, as Mrs. Jefferson Davis, the first lady of the Confederacy, and her children prepared for departure on the evening of March 31, 1865. They arrived at the Richmond railroad station around 8 P.M. and settled into a dilapidated passenger coach. The two youngest children—Billy, age 3, and baby girl Pie—were already asleep when their father came to see them off. Ten-year-old Maggie clung to him all the while he was talking to her mother. Eight-year-old Jeff tried hard not to cry and begged his father to let him remain with him in Richmond—to no avail. When the whistle blew, President Davis kissed the children, embraced his wife, and turned to go. At 10 o'clock, the train lurched forward. Jefferson Davis watched on the station platform until the taillight faded. "He thought he was looking his last upon us," Mrs. Davis later wrote.

The beginning of the end came on April 1, 1865, at the battle of Five Forks, when Sheridan routed a Confederate division, taking nearly five thousand prisoners. Grant promptly ordered an all-out Union attack on the Petersburg line in the early morning of April 2. Relentlessly, his men drove the Confederates out of the trenches. Among the dead left behind were barefoot boys of thirteen and fourteen. "It almost makes one sorry to have to fight against people who show such devotion for their homes and their country," observed one of the Union officers.

The teenager John Sergeant Wise had been in the Confederate army for only ten months when he attained the rank of lieutenant. On April 2 he was at Clover Station, south of Richmond. He had been assigned to an artillery command with orders to defend the Richmond and Danville Railroad line. "Sunday morning broke clear and calm," he remembered. "It was one of the first of those heavenly spring days which to me seem brighter in Virginia than elsewhere." Sitting at the telegraph station, he and his fellow officers waited patiently for news from the front. The telegrams came in rapid succession around eleven o'clock:

> Click-click-click. *"Our lines in front of Petersburg were broken this morning. General Lee is retiring from the city."*
> Click-click-click. *"In the battle of Five Forks which continued until long after dark last night, Pickett was overwhelmed by Sheridan with a greatly superior force of cavalry and infantry."*
> Click-click-click. *"Petersburg is evacuated."*
> Click-click-click. *"General Lee has notified the president that he can no longer hold Richmond, and orders have been issued for the immediate evacuation of the city. The town is the scene of the utmost turmoil and confusion."*

Fourteen-year-old Frances Caldern de la Barca Hunt kept a diary in which she described what happened in Richmond that Sunday:

> April 2nd 1865. *Today is the Sabbath and a very beautiful day it is. It is too beautiful for the impending evil that I felt hovering over us. Flory & I went to church . . . guards were stationed at the church taking up every body that had not a pass. When we came home there were great many rumors afloat, among these were the one which we often hear about, Richmond being evacuated, but we did not believe it as usual.*
>
> *Night came and with it came sorrow and sadness. Cousin Charlie came home and said he would have to go away that night. And then Cousin Willie came and he had to go in the morning. The time came for the sad parting—all was confusion within and without. . . . I retired with a heavy heart for two of my best loved cousins had gone. Perhaps we may never meet again on this earth where nothing but sorrow and sadness reign supreme.*

Like Frances, President Jefferson Davis had attended church services that Sunday morning. While he was there, a sexton handed him a message from General Lee: "My lines are broken in three places, Richmond must be evacuated this evening." Davis left church and ordered that his government move to Danville, Virginia, one hundred forty miles to the southwest. The president boarded the last train out of the city—a series of freight cars labeled "Archives," "Post Office Department," "Treasury Department," "War Department," and so on—a veritable government on wheels.

In the city, chaos reigned. Much of Richmond was set afire by retreating soldiers. Rear Admiral Raphael Semmes blew up all that was left of the

Confederate fleet, anchored in the James River. The shock of the explosion shattered windows throughout the city. Then the fire on land spread to the Confederate arsenal. Young Frances described what it was like:

> April 3rd 1865. *This morning I was awakened from my restless slumber by a loud explosion. I was scared half to death. I thought the Yankees had commenced to bombard the city & they would continue to do all day, but I soon found out . . . our troops were blowing up the magazine to keep the Yankees from getting it. . . . Richmond evacuated, I cannot realize it. . . . All Cory St. is burnt and Maine is on fire, it is spreading rapidly: almost every minute Flory & I are running out to see if the Yankees are coming and if we see them we run as fast as our feet can carry us.*

The news of the fall of the capital of the Confederacy spread rapidly through the countryside. Evelyn Ward heard about it through her cousin Norman, who rode up to her plantation in Westmoreland County. "Yes, he told us, it was true. Richmond had been given up. He told his news manfully, but I never saw a sadder face. . . . He told us of the evacuation: how in places the city had been set afire and the streets ran with whiskey and the liquors that were emptied into them."

Union troops occupied the city on April 3 and did their best to restore order. "Exactly at eight o'clock," a Richmond woman wrote, "the Confederate flag that fluttered above the Capitol came down and the Stars and Stripes were run up. . . . We covered our faces and cried." The next day, Abraham Lincoln and his son Tad arrived at Rockett's Wharf aboard a small barge. "Thank God, I have lived to see this," Lincoln said. "It seems to me that I have been dreaming a horrid nightmare for four years, and now the nightmare is over."

Wrote fourteen-year-old Frances in her diary:

> April 4th. *All is very quiet today. The Yankees are behaving very well considering it is them. . . . I am just as restless as I can be. The negroes of Richmond are delighted. We have no school now and don't know when we will have any. . . . Old Abe has just gotten into the city, & they are firing salutes in honor of his arrival. . . . He first went to the President's house & after leaving, rode around to take a view of Richmond & then went back to the gunboat to stay all night. We have just gotten the evening whig [the local newspaper], it said "that there were from 600 to 800 houses burned". . . . The work of destruction went on until three or four o'clock, then the mastery of the flames was obtained and Richmond was saved from utter desolation.*

A reporter for the *New York World* took a walk through Richmond that evening. He observed, "We are under the shadow of ruins. From the

Ruins of Richmond, Virginia (courtesy of the Library of Congress)

pavements where we walk . . . stretches a vista of devastation. The wreck, the loneliness, seem interminable."

Surrounded by the Yankees who had occupied her city and searched her house, young Frances still had hope that the Confederates *would* prevail. Hope was fed by rumors. She wrote on April 5: "We heard this evening that General Lee had whipped the Yankees and captured a great many prisoners." Nothing could have been further from the truth.

Seventeen-year-old James Lockwood, a drummer boy with the Fourth New York Artillery Regiment, was among the Federal troops who pursued Lee's army on their retreat. He saw daily "thousands of the cavalry captured, and with no apparent unwillingness on their part . . . a discouraged and disheartened lot." He wrote:

The pursuit of Lee's [troops] was little more than a series of hard forced marches, lasting over a week. [We] were constantly passing, upon the roads to Appomattox, abandoned artillery caissons and broken wagons filled with ammunition which were burning. . . . In one instance we captured a large train of wagons . . . the bright new leather of the harness and saddles upon the bony and starving animals which had drawn them looked as if it had never been in a shower of rain; the mules and horses . . . were so exhausted that they could not proceed further and the enemy abandoned them "in park," harnessed and hitched to their . . . wagons and guns, not having time to dismantle or destroy them.

Meanwhile, President Davis, with his provisional government now ensconced in Danville, tried unsuccessfully to communicate with General Lee. The telegraph wires had been cut by Union forces.

Davis asked for a trusted officer who, supplied with an engine, would venture up the railroad line to Burkeville, Virginia, make contact with General Lee, ascertain his situation and future plans, and report back to the president. Lieutenant John Sergeant Wise volunteered. Even though his commanding officer thought him too young for such an important assignment, he was chosen and provided with a tender and baggage car and the services of an engineer.

After a harrowing one-day trip that brought him directly into the lines of the Federal troops, the teenaged lieutenant dismissed engineer and engine and continued northward on horseback. He had found a mare in Meherin, "saddled and bridled as if waiting for me." He later wrote of his adventure, "On the morning of April 6, mounted upon as fine a mare as there was in the Confederacy, I sallied forth in search of General Lee."

That day, Federal forces attacked the remnants of Lee's army at Sailor's Creek. Some eight thousand Confederates were lost or taken prisoner, a third of Lee's army. Sixty-year-old General Henry Wise, the father of young John, was in command that day, and his brigade did some of the best fighting of the war—desperate as it was. Past midnight his son finally found him and General Lee, in an open field near Farmville. John Wise later wrote:

As we passed down the road to General Lee's headquarters, the roads and fields were filled with stragglers. . . . Demoralization, panic, abandonment of all hope, appeared on every hand. . . . Rising to his full height . . . my father exclaimed, "This is the end!"

General Lee asked the young lieutenant to carry a final dispatch back to President Davis at Danville. "When I left him," John Wise wrote, "I felt that I was in the midst of the wreck of that immortal army which, until now, I had believed to be invincible." Two days later, on April 9, Palm Sunday, General Lee surrendered at nearby Appomattox. During the last days of their retreat, his men had been outnumbered nearly four to one, without food or hope of resupply or reinforcement.

News of the surrender spread quickly across the country. Frances Caldern de la Barca Hunt wrote in her diary:

Richmond, April 10, 1865. *Last night heard cannonaiding and [they] said it was either for the capture of General Lee & His army or for Peace. This morning we heard it again. . . . I went round to Mrs. Hughes . . . and there I heard the dreadful news that General Lee had surrendered & then they told me that we were going to have Peace in a very short time. I was pleased but yet I was sad.*

Evelyn Ward of Bladensfield reported: "The next day we heard of the surrender. Poor Mama went to bed and stayed there. All she had lost had been in vain." But seven-year-old Robert Martin of Mount Jackson felt a great burden lifted from his small shoulders: "When the news came of the surrender at Appomattox and this was the end and that it also meant the return of my father whom I can recall seeing not more than twice during the war, I rejoiced inwardly with a great and exceeding joy."

Guns saluted the news of Appomattox in Washington, D.C., on April 10, one week after the jubilation over the fall of Richmond. "Let Master Tad [Lincoln's son] have a Navy sword," the president directed, and he added in a note to the Secretary of War: "Tad wants some flags. Can he be accommodated?" A couple of hours later, the boy stood at a second-story window of the White House and waved a captured Confederate flag to the wild applause of a crowd of thousands.

Presently his father appeared at the window, and the yells grew louder. "I see you have a band of music with you," Lincoln said, and he asked that the musicians play "a particular tune which I will name. . . . I have always thought 'Dixie' one of the best tunes I ever heard. . . . I now request the band to favor me with its performance."

The next night, Lincoln was back at the window with Tad by his side; again the boy was waving a Confederate banner. "Fellow Citizens," he said, "We are met this evening not in sorrow but in gladness of heart. The evacuation of Petersburg and Richmond, and the surrender of the principal insurgent army, gives hope of a righteous and speedy peace whose joyous expression cannot be restrained." Lincoln went on with his speech, dropping each read page on the balcony floor. Tad scrambled about to catch the sheets as they fluttered down. "Another, another," he kept saying all through his father's reading. The crowd heard it plainly as a hush descended on the audience on the White House lawn.

When the news of Lee's surrender reached the Union forces in the field, there was rejoicing everywhere—from camps in Alabama to Tennessee, from Georgia to North Carolina. The drummer boys and the fifers struck up a lively tune, and the men cheered until they grew hoarse. Pri-

Tad Lincoln in a colonel's uniform (courtesy of the National Archives)

vate Elisha Stockwell was marching with his Wisconsin company toward Montgomery, Alabama, when "we got the news that Lee had surrendered." Their celebration was a noisy one:

> *They lined up the artillery of the whole command and fired a gun just about as fast as one could count. An officer sat on a horse at the right of the gun, and he had a small flag. . . . Every time he made a motion down a gun was fired. So the firing was as regular as a clock. This sounded nice to us as it was the death knell of the secession and meant the cruel war was over.*

Theodore Upson was with his Indiana regiment in Goldsborough, North Carolina, when on April 12 they received the word that Lee had surrendered. "Our boys hardly believed it at first," he wrote in his diary. But then they had a great blowout at the headquarters of his commanding general:

> *He had a great big bowl sitting on a camp table. . . . The General handed me a tin cup. "Help yourself," said he. I dipped in, took a little drink, handed it to*

the other boys. . . . General Woods . . . made a little speech, telling us Rich-mond was ours, that Lee and his Army had surrendered, that it was the end of the war, and that we should celebrate as we had never done before. . . .

After a while a Band came. They played once or twice, drank some, played some more, then drank some more of that never ending supply of punch, then they played again but did not keep very good time. Some of them could not wait till they got through with a tune till they had to pledge Grant and his gallant Army, also Lee and his grand fighters. . . . The Band finally got so they were trying to play two or three tunes at once. Then the General realized that they were very tired, and he would relieve them. He got the big drum, other officers took the various horns—every fellow blowing his horn to suit himself and the jolly old general pounding the bass drum for all it was worth. . . . Some sang or tried to sing, but when "Johnny Comes Marching Home," and "John Brown's Body" or "Hail Columbia" and the "Star Spangled Banner" are all sung together they get mixed so I don't really think the singing was a grand success from an artistic standpoint . . . but it let out a lot of pent up exuberant feeling that had to have an outlet.

Four days after Lee's surrender, on April 14, 1865, Good Friday, Lincoln was shot by John Wilkes Booth at the Ford Theater in Washington, D.C. He died early the next morning. The news of the assassination stunned the country. The drummer boy William Bircher from Minnesota observed: "The dark pall of sorrow hung over the army today. The whole army wept." But sorrow was mixed with feelings of anger. Theodore Upson wrote, "We have just received the terrible news. . . . The men are fearfully angry and I don't know what they may do. I have had orders to keep my guards together. It is said some of the troops intend to burn and sack Raleigh [North Carolina]."

Revenge was also on the mind of seventeen-year-old Emma LeConte from Columbia, South Carolina:

Hurrah! Old Abe has been assassinated! It may be abstractly wrong to be so jubilant, but I just can't help it. . . . This blow to our enemies comes like a gleam of light. We have suffered till we feel savage. . . . The first feeling I had when the news were announced was simply gratified revenge. The man we hated has met his proper fate. . . . What exciting, what eventful times we are living in!

Not everyone in the South greeted Lincoln's death with "a spirit of reckless hate." In Bladensfield, Virginia, Evelyn Ward remembered "everyone talking about it, and reading the papers when any were to be had, and my Father saying, 'In him the South has lost her best friend in the North.'"

On April 26, 1865, Confederate General Joseph Johnston formally surrendered what remained of his Army of Tennessee to Sherman. The Georgia girl Eliza Andrews witnessed the disintegration of the Confederate armies and the homecoming of the soldiers:

> *The shattered remains . . . are beginning to arrive. . . . Our avenue leads from the principal street on which they pass, and a great number stop to rest in the grove. Emily is kept busy cooking rations for them, and pinched as we are ourselves for supplies, it is impossible to refuse anything to the men that have been fighting for us. Even when they don't ask for anything, the poor fellows look so tired and hungry that we feel tempted to give them everything we have.*

A good many Union soldiers shared Eliza's compassion. The teenager John Sergeant Wise was traveling back by train to Richmond, the brass buttons on his lieutenant's uniform covered with black as a badge of mourning for the dead Confederacy. The cars were crowded with Union soldiers who were, he noticed, "extremely civil and conciliatory." He remembered:

> *One fellow was so kind that, after he had offered me money, which I refused, he slipped it into my pocket, with a card saying, "This is not a gift, but a loan, and when you are able you can return it to me." . . . I never forgot his delicate attention.*

John Wise found a temporary abode with his brother-in-law. There he received a package of civilian clothing from his Philadelphia relatives who had known him only as a boy. "When I looked in the glass," he noticed, "instead of confronting a striking young officer, I beheld a mere insignificant bit of an eighteen-year-old boy. I had received a great set back in manhood." The next morning, after a sleepless night, he composed his will:

> *I, J. Reb, being of unsound mind and bitter memory, and aware that I am dead, do make public and declare the following to be my political last will and testament.*
>
> *I give, device, and bequeath all my slaves to Harriet Beecher Stowe.*
>
> *I direct that all my shares in the venture of secession shall be cancelled, provided I am released from my unpaid subscription to the stock of said enterprise.*
>
> *My interest in the civil government of the Confederacy I bequeath to any freak museum that may hereafter be established.*
>
> *My sword, my veneration for General Robert E. Lee, his subordinate commanders and his peerless soldiers, and my undying love for my old*

comrades, living and dead, I set apart as the best I have, or shall ever have, to bequeath to my heirs forever.

And now, being dead, having experienced a death to Confederate ideas and a new birth unto allegiance to the Union, I depart, with a vague but not definite hope of a joyful resurrection, and of a new life, upon lines somewhat different from those of the last eighteen years. I see what has been pulled down very clearly. What is to be built up in its place I know not. It is a mystery; but death is always mysterious. AMEN.

Some Confederate diehards *did* fight on in Alabama, Louisiana, Mississippi, and Texas. The final skirmish on May 13 at Palmito Ranch, Texas, was a victory for the South!

Ten days later, on the morning of May 23, 1865, General Grant and Andrew Johnson, the new president, stood side by side to watch the Grand Armies of the Republic pass in review down Pennsylvania Avenue from the capitol in Washington, D.C. It took two full days for the one hundred fifty thousand men to march by. Among the marchers were four teenage boys who had enlisted when they were barely fifteen: William Bircher, the drummer boy from Minnesota; Leverett Bradley, from the First Massachusetts Heavy Artillery; Theodore Gerrish, a private from Maine; and Theodore Upson, now a sergeant in the Hundredth Indiana Infantry.

Theodore Gerrish and Leverett Bradley marched on the first day in the Grand Army of the Potomac, under the command of John Wise's uncle, General George Meade—with the effortless discipline mastered on a hundred marches from Bull Run to Appomattox. They wore new uniforms and white gloves. Remembered Theodore Gerrish:

We were tired and worn from the long weary marches we had made but it was not a difficult task to get up considerable enthusiasm . . . hundreds of school children, all dressed in white . . . hurled . . . beautiful bouquets of flowers upon us as we passed; the bands all played the national airs; the people cheered until they were hoarse; banners waved and handkerchiefs fluttered.

Leverett Bradley wrote to his family:

The great review has passed. It was a beautiful day. I was the left guide of the color company; many were the remarks about our tattered banners. The ladies kept their handkerchiefs going all the time. . . . The streets were crowded full to overflowing.

William Bircher and Theodore Upson paraded on the second day in the Army of the West. They marched with a looser stride than their eastern counterparts and wore loose shirts and soft hats rather than crisp uniforms. General Sherman himself, with his battered slouch hat, rode at the head of the great army he had led to the sea. Noted William Bircher in his diary:

We marched down Pennsylvania Avenue, on which every house was beautifully decorated with buntings, streamers and flags, flying from every window and housetop. The people were wild with enthusiasm.

Observed Theodore Upson, "When we passed the Reviewing Stand . . . all the great men of the nation . . . rose to their feet and with bared heads cheered and cheered. I glanced down the line of our platoon—every man had his eyes front, every step was perfect; and on the faces of the men was . . . a glory look."

There were no black troops in the victory parade.

The boy John Wise from Virginia was a visitor at the home of his uncle, General Meade, in Philadelphia, when he witnessed the triumphant return of the victorious Union armies. He was regarded by his relatives as such a mere child that he was not invited to the table when company came, but dined with other children in the nursery. That summer he fished, in overalls and a straw hat, near the shores of Chesapeake Bay. In September 1865, he went back to school. A few of his classmates remembered that he had once been a proud lieutenant in the Provisional Army of the Confederate States of America.

EPILOGUE

I am "young" and politics are conducted by "grown-ups." But I think the "young" would do it better. We certainly would not have chosen war.

Zlata Filipovic, age eleven, of Sarajevo

ON CHRISTMAS EVE 1865, Carrie Berry walked to Sunday School in her hometown of Atlanta. The city had slowly risen from the ashes. After years of wartime privations, the young girl was looking forward to the few simple gifts—apples, nuts, a piece of candy—she would receive the next morning.

Most of the boy soldiers from the North had gone back home—to the midwestern towns and northeastern cities they had left more than four years ago. Elisha Stockwell was farming in Wisconsin. William Bircher was working in a saloon known as "Billy Bircher's Place" in St. Paul, Minnesota. Thomas Galwey and James Newton were attending college in Ohio. In time, Galwey would become a lawyer and editor and a professor of Logic, Latin, and French literature at Manhattan College in New York. Newton would teach German and French at Oberlin College, Ohio.

Theodore Gerrish from Maine would become a minister who preached the gospel of peace to his flock. The Hoosier boy Theodore Upson would build fine carriages, wagons, and sleighs, and the drummer boy Cordy Foote would open a tinshop that flourished. Johnny Clem would become a career officer in the U.S. Army.

The teenage survivors of Andersonville would spend a lifetime telling others about their stay in hell. In 1866, while the horrors of the camp were still fresh on his mind, John McElroy, now a printer and newspaperman, wrote a series of articles about his experiences as a prisoner of war for the *Toledo Blade*.

Two years later, in the winter of 1868, Billy Bates, who had graduated from college at Ann Arbor, Michigan, gave his first talk, entitled "From Andersonville Prison to the White House," in Cleveland, Ohio. Until his death in 1909, he lectured to school children all over the country, from the Atlantic to the Pacific.

Trimming the Christmas tree, 1865 (courtesy of the Allison-Shelley Collection, the Pennsylvania State University Libraries)

Michael Dougherty, the sole survivor among the men in his regiment held captive in Andersonville, was awarded the Congressional Medal of Honor for "most distinguished gallantry in action" thirty-two years after the Civil War had ended. His account, *Prison Diary*, was published in 1908.

William Smith lost the use of his lower limbs from a spinal disease contracted at Andersonville and was strapped to a wheelchair for most of his life. In 1881 he moved with his family to Florida, where he counted among his friends many old Confederate soldiers. In 1892 he published a book with the whimsical title *On wheels and How I Came There—a Real Story for Real Boys and Girls*. On the front page of his memoirs is the Biblical admonition "Neither shall they learn war any more." Prophet Isaiah's plea was not heeded by the civilized world: Fifty years after his book was published, World War II raged in Europe, and the concentration camps of Auschwitz, Belsen-Bergen, and Buchenwald were in full operation.

The boys of the Confederacy returned to ruined cities and a countryside ravaged by the war. Texas bugler Albert Blocker settled on a plantation that once belonged to a family of slaveholders and worked the land together with his new bride. George Gibbs, the beardless boy from Mississippi, survived four years of desperate combat and emerged from the Lost Cause a man of twenty, minus a leg, but otherwise strong and wise beyond his years. His reminiscences, written after the war for his children, show a man of integrity, with a fine sense of humor.

Two of the teenage officers from the Confederacy, Lieutenant John Sergeant Wise from Virginia and Captain William H.S. Burgwyn from North Carolina, became well-respected lawyers. So did the boy soldier Henry Clay Rooney who had been wounded at Gettysburg; he would become a district judge in Augusta, Georgia.

The boy Robert Hugh Martin who had watched some of the last skirmishes of the Civil War from the front porch of his home near Mount Jackson, Virginia, would, in time, become a teacher, school principal, and newspaper editor. Henry Morton Stanley, who had his baptism of fire at Shiloh, never lost his yearning for adventure. He became a correspondent and world traveler whose exploits included tracking down the explorer David Livingstone in Central Africa.

Many of the former boy soldiers, both in the North and South, became active in local politics and participated in city, state, and national government in elective or appointed positions. William Bircher first became city clerk in St. Paul, Minnesota, and later, in his retirement, mayor of St. Cloud, Florida. Thomas Galwey was appointed city attorney of New York, Henry Clay Rooney served as legislator in the Georgia General Assembly, and John S. Wise was a candidate from Virginia for the United States Senate.

Most of the young girls who witnessed the devastation of the South went back to school when the war was over and resumed their studies. They married men who had been veterans of the Lost Cause and wrote down their childhood memories of the war for their children and grand-children. Eliza Andrews, who had pitied the Yankee prisoners of Andersonville, would become a teacher and write novels and scientific books. Mary Loughborough, who had endured the siege of Vicksburg with her little girl, founded one of the nation's first magazines for women, the *Arkansas Ladies Journal*.

Emma LeConte, who had once thought her world had ended with Lee's surrender, would as a young widow manage her own plantation and become active in the suffragette movement. Among her church-related activities was assisting at a school for black children. She lived long enough to see women gain the vote and a seat in the U.S. House of Representatives. The Civil War had transformed her and many other Southern girls of her social standing from delicate dependents on their menfolk to resilient survivors who managed their businesses, farms, and households with enterprise, fortitude, and fierce pride.

Some of the most remarkable transformations took place among the young girls who had been eyewitnesses to the emancipation of Southern slaves. Seventeen-year-old Susie King was left alone with her baby to fend for herself when her husband died shortly after the end of the Civil War. Within a year, she opened a school for freedmen in Liberty County, Georgia, and then a night school for adults in Savannah. With an income of one dollar a month for each pupil, she supported herself and her child.

Mattie Jackson, the ex-slave from Missouri, settled in Lawrence, Kansas, after the Civil War had ended. She told the story of her escape from slavery to a friend who wrote it down and edited it for her. The preface of her autobiography, published in 1866, reads: "I ask you to buy my little book to aid me in obtaining my education that I may be enabled to do some good on behalf of the elevation of my emancipated brothers and sisters." She spent a lifetime introducing others to the magic of a scrap of writing.

Ex-slaves who had been children during "the War Between the States" and the drummer boys, because of their youth, came to be the last sur-vivors of the Civil War. Most lived well into their eighties and nineties. Johnny Clem died in 1937 at the age of eighty-five. Cordy Foote died in 1944 at the age of ninety-five. During his long life he saw American soldiers march off to two World Wars on foreign soil.

Memories of the Civil War are still kept alive today by the descendants of those who fought it—especially in the South. In September 1996, more than one hundred thirty years after the last shot was fired in the American Civil War, the first African American chairman of the Joint Chiefs of Staff,

General Colin Powell, spoke at a dedication service for a Civil War Monument honoring the 185,000 black soldiers and sailors and their white officers who had served the Union in that bloody conflict. "This memorial links us to our past," he said. "It recovers our history for all of us to see."

One month later, in October 1996, the state of Alabama awarded a pension to eighty-nine-year-old Alberta Martin, recognizing her as the "Confederacy's Last Widow." At the age of twenty-one, she had become the third wife of William Jasper Martin, age eighty-one, who had served as a boy soldier in the Fourth Alabama Infantry Regiment during the bloody ten-month struggle for Petersburg, Virginia, in 1864 and 1865.

On July 1, 1997, Alberta Martin met Daisy Anderson, age ninety-six, widow of a black union soldier, in Gettysburg at a burial ceremony for an unknown Civil War soldier whose remains were found the year before in the battlefield. They shook hands, embraced, and together placed roses on the soldier's coffin at Gettysburg National Cemetery. They had come to bury the past.

The passions stirred by that distant American Armageddon still reverberate around the world today. The Civil War was the first modern war, and for the United States, the costliest in casualties and domestic sufferings. It was a total war that involved millions of noncombatants—the opening chapter in a continuing series of conflicts around the globe in which increasing numbers of casualties, both physical and psychological, are children.

In the wars of the nineteenth and early twentieth centuries, about half the victims were civilians. Since World War II the proportion of civilian casualties—especially child casualties—has been rising steadily. In World War II, two-thirds of the killed and maimed were civilians. Nine out of ten of the casualties of contemporary civil wars in Africa, Asia, Europe, and Latin America are now noncombatants—mostly women and children.[1]

The trauma of exposure to prolonged violence has emotionally affected several generations of children and young people. In World War II alone, millions of children were uprooted and were denied the physical and emotional security they had once taken for granted. Children came to know the horrors of the Holocaust, of saturation bombings, and of hunger and starvation, and they were witnesses to murder, rape, and death.

Since the end of World War II more than one hundred armed conflicts have been fought on four continents. Civil wars have torn whole countries apart—from Afghanistan to Cambodia, from Bosnia-Herzegovina to Ethiopia and Rwanda, from Northern Ireland to Lebanon. Everywhere, the children of war gaze at us with eyes that have seen a lifetime of suffering.[2]

The steady rise in child casualties in these armed conflicts is in part a function of the technology of modern wars. Aerial bombardment has extended the potential battlezone to the towns and cities of entire nations.

The children of World War II saw a massive increase in indiscriminate killing with the bombings of Coventry, Hamburg, and Dresden and the atomic bombs dropped on Hiroshima and Nagasaki. Additionally today, there is a steady proliferation of light weapons that are lethal, from "Molotov cocktails" to assault rifles and shoulder-held missiles.

Most child casualties in modern wars are civilians, but an alarming increase in the number of child soldiers has also taken place. There are now hundreds of thousands of children under the age of sixteen, some as young as six, who have fought in far-flung places from Angola to Mozambique and from Burma to Peru.[3] Their assault rifles are lightweight and simple to use. They can be stripped and reassembled by a child of ten. Had Thomas Galwey or Elisha Stockwell lived and fought today they would be experts in handling these small arms. So would a modern-day Susie King, for among guerrillas in civil wars from Asia and Central America to Africa and the Middle East are now an increasing number of young girls.

The duties of child soldiers in modern civil wars cover the whole range of military activities. In quiet times in camp, they may help with food preparation or carrying water, just as the drummer boys did in the American Civil War. Being small and inconspicuous, children are also valued as messengers or as spies. But often they are *also* considered the most expendable among the warring factions. During the Iran-Iraq war, for example, waves of child soldiers were sent out ahead of regular troops to clear the minefields.

The political violence that has swept across the world in recent years has uprooted more than fifty million people—at least half of whom are children. Some have fled their homes to move elsewhere within their own country, as many Southern families did in the wake of Sherman's march to the sea. Others have crossed borders into neighboring countries where they are not welcome.

Poor housing and poor nutrition are part of a war refugee's life. The Confederate widow from Fredericksburg who found temporary abode in a cold room in Richmond and fed her three children an occasional meal of turnip tops knew that. So did Céline Frémaux from Baton Rouge when she fled with her six young siblings to the Louisiana countryside.

Whether they are on their own or with their parents, most of the children who die in wartime are not killed by bombs or bullets but by contagious diseases and hunger. Among those who survive, millions have witnessed events far beyond the worst nightmares of most adults.

Whether they live in Angola, Cambodia, Vietnam, or Sarajevo, almost all child survivors of modern wars have been in situations where they thought they might be killed by snipers, shells, or bombs, and all have seen dead or maimed bodies—of family members, neighbors, friends, or the enemy.[4] If they could reach across the centuries, the children of Baton Rouge, Fredericksburg, and Gettysburg could comprehend the nightmares of their modern peers. They, too, remembered for a lifetime the sight of body parts strewn in the streets of their hometowns, of decomposing corpses and grinning skulls.

> *A grenade had landed on our shelter. We had to climb over the dead bodies to get out. Meanwhile the snipers kept shooting at us. . . . I try not to talk about these things, but I get so upset and keep having nightmares about what happened.*

Young Lucy McRae from Vicksburg would have understood thirteen-year-old Kazimir from Sarajevo, who wrote these lines in 1994. One hundred and thirty years earlier she, too, had climbed out of the rubble of a collapsed cellar under a hail of gunfire and had narrowly escaped death.

Every armed conflict forces children to live through some terrible experiences. Since World War II, physicians and mental health professionals have observed a wide range of symptoms among the child survivors of modern wars—not unlike those reported by soldiers who fought on the front lines.[5] Memories of the traumatic events remain with them, causing nightmares, flashbacks, and hypersensitivity to sights, smells, and sounds that remind them of their wartime experiences: the sound of an exploding shell; the whistling of a bomb, the sparks of fire; the smell of burning wood; the unexpected knock at the door or a uniform that may evoke the memory of an enemy who might seize one's parents or one's earthly possessions.

Some horrific war experiences are so overwhelming that children may try to suppress their memories rather than confront them. But time does not heal such trauma unless it *is* confronted. The very act of talking or writing about it is a way for child survivors of wars to begin the healing process. The children and teenagers who wrote about their experiences in the American Civil War may have already discovered that road to recovery. Some of their most vivid eyewitness accounts were perhaps more than the mere telling of an exciting tale to their family and friends—they may have been a way to mend themselves and to put together the pieces of their shattered lives.[6]

The trauma of war appears to affect children differently, depending on the level of violence they have been exposed to and their capacity to cope with it. The effects tend to vary also with their age, gender, and temperament; their family and social support; and the political ideology or religious faith that provides context in their lives.

Studies of child survivors of contemporary wars suggest that those youngsters are most likely to be traumatized who have witnessed violence against family members, suffered violence themselves, experienced loss or bereavement, and lacked the support of their family and community. Several accounts in this book give a hint of experiences that made some of the youngest children especially vulnerable to the vagaries of the Civil War. Pregnant Betty Herndon Maury had fled Fredericksburg with her five-year-old daughter after the bombardments in December 1862. She was living in a rented room in Richmond, with no news from her husband, who was in the Confederate army, and no extended family to fall back on for support. In her diary the young mother worried about the fears and nightmares of her daughter, who was afraid of strangers and loud noises that reminded her of events that had taken place during the siege of Fredericksburg.

Mary Loughborough's two-year-old daughter was in similar distress during the bombardment of Vicksburg in 1863. She slept little and would cling to her mother's skirt when shells fell near her cave. Then cautiously looking out, she would ask, "Was it a mortal tell?" The little girl's distress increased when, a few days later, she witnessed how an exploded shell took off the hands of a soldier who had befriended her.

Young children seem to be especially vulnerable to parental distress during bombing raids and prolonged shelling. British and German children who lived through prolonged aerial attacks in World War II, for example, were more disturbed by the anxiety of their parents than by the actual severity of the bombings.

Eighty years earlier, Dora Miller saw in Vicksburg just how contagious a mother's fears could be. A shell had exploded in her garden, and three or four pieces had penetrated the kitchen walls. Her cook screamed, ashen faced, "My child is killed." The cook's daughter was bleeding from a slight wound in the forehead but responding to her mother's anxiety, "was fairly dancing with fright and uttering fearful yells." And four-year-old Lida Lord watching her mother's horror-stricken reaction to the explosion of two bombshells near the entrance of their cellar sobbed with fright and worried that god had been killed, too.

One of the most distressing war traumas of all, particularly for young children, is simply separation from their parents—often more distressing than the violence that surrounds them. Kati David was five years old and living with her Jewish family in Amsterdam when World War II began. In her book, *A Child's War*, she vividly remembered the terror of separation:

> *Once, when I heard my father say that he was considering sending only us children into hiding because he did not have enough savings to pay for all of us, I panicked. Being left behind and having to live with other people seemed to me the worst thing of all. I was much more afraid of that than being sent to a camp with my parents. . . . All that did not seem so terrible as long as we could stay together as a family.*[7]

Few of the children on the home front were separated from their immediate families during the American Civil War, but even a temporary separation from her parents during the battle of Gettysburg brought anxiety to Jeannie McCreary, who was hiding in a neighbor's cellar. We can only wonder about the state of mind of the two little girls from Georgia, age three and five, who were found, without a trace of their parents, by a foraging party from Sherman's army during their march to the sea. They were mute. No one knew what horrors they had seen.

Fortunately, most of the young eyewitnesses who told about their experiences in the American Civil War could count on the protection of a caring family member—a mother, grandmother, or older sister. Given that security, some youngsters reacted to the sights and sounds of the war with curiosity, excitement, and even a sense of adventure. Their tender age and lack of experience limited their ability to envision the inherent uncertainties and imminent dangers of war.

Many of the youngest children were intrigued by shells and weapons and fascinated by gunfire and bombing. During the siege of Vicksburg, Fanny Russell, who was less than five years at the time, would go out with some slave girls a little older than herself and pick up minie balls. "Even when shelling was in progress," she remembered, "we were at our posts to pick up the pieces of shell as soon as they were cold enough." That pastime also amused a fair-haired three-year-old girl in Fredericksburg who, during the bombardment of the city, pursued the exploding shells in the company of her Newfoundland dog, unaware of the danger she was exposed to.

The young boys at Gettysburg fancied swords and unexploded shells as well. On the first day of the battle, ten-year-old Charles McCurdy wandered into the deserted camp of the Federal cavalry and spent precious time tugging away at a small sword that had been driven into the ground. He clung to it, even as heavy cannons began to boom nearby, but had to finally abandon the weapon as it proved to be too much of a burden in his flight from the artillery fire.

The majority of the children who wrote about their experiences in the Civil War were older than Fanny Russell or Lida Lord or Charlie McCurdy. Most were in their early and middle teens. Like many youngsters caught in the turmoil of contemporary wars, they had their own spontaneous way of making sense of the chaos they lived through. Over time, both the children on the home front and the boy soldiers revealed a growing sense of competence and confidence, even in the midst of danger to themselves and the people they cared for.

Surrounded by death and destruction, these youngsters were able to draw on the sustained emotional support of members of their extended family, of friends and neighbors, and in the case of the boy soldiers, of comrades in their regiment. But they also gave something in return: They assumed responsibilities that were essential to the well-being and survival of their families or fighting units. This experience bolstered their self-confidence and morale and strengthened their belief that they *could* survive.[8] Rarely, even when in acute physical danger or in the face of impending defeat, did they loose hope.

A contemporary reader may well be astounded at the responsibilities assumed by these children: Ten-year-old Carrie Berry, during the siege and burning of Atlanta, took care of a household that consisted of a pregnant mother and a sickly younger sister. After her mother had given birth to a baby girl, Carrie cooked, cleaned, sewed clothing for the family, and took care of her baby sister as well. After her hometown was burned, she and other young children scrounged through the ruins picking up nails and lead to trade for a bit of food. Yet she never lost a child's enthusiasm and joy of life! She was grateful for a lull in the shelling, for the large cellar in which she could romp about and her family could securely hide, and for a little Christmas tree that she could decorate in the ruins of her burned-out city.

In like manner twelve-year-old Céline Frémaux during the bombardment of Baton Rouge and the siege of Port Hudson showed herself entirely capable of taking care of six younger siblings, including a newborn baby brother. "In these few months," she later wrote, "my childhood had slipped away from me. . . . Necessity, human obligations, family pride and patriotism had taken entire possession of my little emaciated body."

Equally remarkable was the sense of responsibility and competence displayed by fourteen-year-old Susie King, who started a school for ex-slaves on San Simeon Island, taught both children and adults how to read, and nursed the wounded soldiers in her husband's regiment. She also learned how to handle a musket and never missed her target.

Northern children, like Maria Lewis from Ebensburg, Pennsylvania, took on adult responsibilities as well, helping their mothers take care of younger siblings and the family farm when their fathers left to fight for the Union. And in Gettysburg, in the midst of a raging battle, youngsters in their early and middle teens ventured forth to take care of injured soldiers, binding their wounds and comforting them as best they could. "I never thought I could do anything about a wounded man," wrote Jeannie McCreary after the battle was over, "but find that I had a little bit more nerve than I thought I had."

So did the fourteen- and fifteen-year-old drummer boys, like Charles Bardeen and William Bircher, who under fire, went out to the battlefields of Fredericksburg and Gettysburg to rescue the wounded and to bury the dead. Many of the boy soldiers on both sides of the Civil War had grown up on farms and knew how to do a man's work by the time they were in their early teens. Now they did a soldier's work, courageously and uncomplaining, in the midst of enemy fire.

Generally, those boy soldiers who held up best under the war's adversities were active and outgoing youngsters, like ten-year-old Johnny Clem, who "was a bright, cheery child," and twelve-year-old Johnnie Walker, who "was liked by everybody in his regiment." Even in the Andersonville prison, the boy soldiers who managed to survive tended to be—according to a teenage observer—"youths who were quick, active and of a cheerful disposition," like the drummer boy nicknamed Red Cap. Such outgoing youngsters attracted the attention and affection of both officers and fellow soldiers—and occasionally even of the enemy.

Many boy soldiers found an "adult" protector in their regiment who looked out after them. Some served with relatives in the same company: Twelve-year-old Johnnie Walker had a half-brother who was a sergeant in his regiment; sixteen-year-old Ed Spangler served with his eighteen-year-old brother Fred in the same company. The fifteen-year-old drummer boy William Bircher and his father were assigned to the same Minnesota regiment, and the fifteen-year-old sailor from the USS *Water Witch* who ended up in Andersonville was looked after by an older shipmate. "Uncle Billy" Sherman was the ultimate father figure for the teenage drummers and fifers who marched with him to the sea.

For children who lived at home in the besieged cities of the South, from Baton Rouge to Vicksburg, from Atlanta to Columbia, teachers were often a valued source of emotional support. Most of the girls who kept a diary of their wartime experiences mention a favorite teacher who insisted that they keep up with their studies, often at great personal cost. Céline Frémaux walked to school across Baton Rouge surrounded by the sounds of gunfire from the riverboats and the sight and smell of decaying bodies. Carrie Berry kept up with her spelling lessons throughout the siege and shelling of Atlanta. Emma LeConte tutored her younger sister amidst the rubble of Columbia, South Carolina.

Books became a refuge for youngsters who sat for days and weeks in dark cellars, listening to the whistling of bombs and shells. Dora Miller kept up her courage in Vicksburg by reading Charles Dickens's stories. In Columbia, Emma LeConte, in the fourth year of the Civil War, wrote in her diary: "If it had not been for my books [the war] would, indeed, have been hard to bear. But in them I have lived and found my chief source of pleasure. I would take refuge in them from the sadness all around."

In camp or prison, books sustained the boy soldiers as well. They carried books in their knapsacks and read them until the leaves fell apart. Boys who owned a Bible, like Ed Spangler, shared it with others as they made ready for battle. And they sang hymns to keep up their morale—the children in the caves of Vicksburg, and the teenage prisoners in Andersonville.

Sometimes, in the darkest hours of the Civil War, the children experienced the unexpected kindness of strangers. Compassion was not extinguished by gunfire and shells: A Confederate sharpshooter risked his life to save the three-year-old girl who ran after the exploding shells on the streets of Fredericksburg. A Union soldier shared his meager rations with a seventeen-year-old Confederate widow whose baby was hungry. Another, a Quaker by persuasion, rescued the meager belongings of a ten-year-old girl from her collapsing home during the burning of Columbia. A party of Sherman's foragers adopted two little orphans on their march to the sea.

And up North, tired and hungry Confederate soldiers shared molasses candies with the children of Gettysburg and saw to it that some of the families they befriended in the evenings, after the roar of the battle died down, were transported safely across their lines and out of harm's way.

The boy soldiers on the battlefields grew used to death and destruction, but they remained sensitive to individual suffering among their comrades and among their adversaries as well. At Sharpsburg, fifteen-year-old Thomas Galwey stooped under fire to give a wounded Southerner a drink of water from his canteen. At Gettysburg, on the third and bloodiest day of the battle, Galwey watched a similar act of kindness extended by a Confederate sharpshooter to a wounded Union soldier. And both sides cheered the teenage Sergeant Richard Kirkland from South Carolina, who risked his life bringing water to the wounded and dying at Mary's Heights in Fredericksburg.

The boy soldiers of the Civil War were still aware of the humanity of their "enemies," who were barely older than themselves. At Shiloh, in his first battle, sixteen-year-old John A. Cockerill wept at the sight of the corpse of a "beautiful boy in grey . . . who was about my age." And fifteen-year-old William Bircher thought of the sorrows and tears that would be shed not only in the North but also "in the far off South."

During the siege of Vicksburg, two teenage soldiers from Wisconsin, Elisha Stockwell and James Newton, worried about the children who might be hurt by the shells that were raining down on the beleaguered city. After the burning of Atlanta, the Hoosier boy Theodore Upson thought it "pretty tough to rout people out of their homes." And when Columbia went up in flames, he and his comrades tried to do all in their power to help the stricken people. "We were *not* fighting children," he wrote to his parents.

Observations of contemporary children who live in war zones show that they, too, have not lost their sensitivity to other people's suffering, even the enemy's. That was especially true for the children of World War II. Observed a ten-year-old English boy when German prisoners were brought to England: "To discover that people I feared and hated—that I had been *taught* to fear and hate—were just like us—and not at all the gruesome, terrifying enemies one heard talk about—was one of my first lessons in understanding people."

Perhaps the children of war, across the centuries, can perceive more clearly our shared humanity than the adults who declare the wars. Close up, from a height of four or five feet, the enemy looks like another human being, not like an anonymous blip on a radar screen.

Some of the most remarkable testimony to human resilience comes from the eyewitness reports of the youngsters who survived their stay in Andersonville. Many were underage—some were only twelve years old. The narrators of this awesome tale—Billy Bates, Michael Dougherty, John McElroy, and William Smith—were in their mid-teens when they were taken prisoner. They survived because they never lost hope and because they were sustained by the support of their comrades and their faith.

The protective factors that seem to have made a difference between survival and death in the camp were very similar to those reported in two mid-life follow-up studies of youngsters who were imprisoned during and after World War II. Among them were the child survivors of concentration camps whose stories were told by Sarah Moskovitz in her book *Love Despite Hate* and the offspring of guerrilla fighters who spent their earliest years with their mothers in a maximum security prison during the Greek Civil War.[9] Mando Dalianis, a pediatrician and child psychiatrist, took care of their medical needs while she was a fellow prisoner and followed them in mid-life when most had grown into caring, competent, and confident adults.[10]

The most striking qualities shared by these child survivors of modern wars was an affirmation of life, an active compassion for others in need, and a sense of belonging provided by their peers or by their religious faith—as well as small acts of kindness from strangers. These themes also resonate in the eyewitness reports of the boys from Andersonville.

All of the survivors made a deliberate decision *not* to lose hope in the face of seemingly insurmountable adversity and set about filling each prison day with activities that affirmed life: sharing scarce food and water with their fellow prisoners, nursing the sick and wounded, and engaging in activities that would sharpen their wits—all the while being sustained by their religious faith or a fervent belief in the cause they had fought for.

The common thread that runs from the eyewitness accounts of the boys in Andersonville to the stories of the child survivors of the Holocaust and the Greek Civil War is the impact of a few caring persons in their lives: the prison priest and the Sisters of Charity who tended to the needs of the sick and wounded in Andersonville; the teachers who mended the spirits of the child survivors of the concentration camps; and the Greek "godmothers"—women prisoners who shared food and clothing with the imprisoned children, played with them, sang with them, and taught them how to read.

Across the centuries, from the boy soldiers of Andersonville to the children of Theresienstadt, Auschwitz, and Averof Prison, the resilient survivors preserved, against all odds, one of the most essential criteria for humanness—the ability to behave compassionately. Maltreatment and malnutrition may have stunted their physical growth or maimed their bodies, but it did not kill their spirit.

The youngsters who witnessed the horrors of the Civil War and lived to tell their tales are but a small sample of the children whose lives were touched by that bloody conflict. They were intelligent and perceptive and had the talent and inclination to write down their experiences so they and the people they cared for would not forget.

There were many other children who witnessed this American tragedy but who remained silent or were rendered mute. None of the boys who were massacred by Confederate guerrillas in Quantrill's raids could tell us what it was like to be shot down—execution style—on the streets of Lawrence, Kansas, on August 21, 1863, during a three-hour orgy of destruction.

The Arapahoe babies and the Cheyenne toddlers at Sand Creek cried when their hapless families were attacked by a band of Colorado Volunteers in Union uniform on a wintry November morning in 1864. But they could not tell us what it was like to be clubbed and shot to death, like fleeing rabbits, and then to be scalped and mutilated for good measure. "Nits make lice," the commander of the Coloradans, Colonel John M. Chivington, had said to justify the killing.

Thousands of boy soldiers, Union and Confederate, who were killed on the battlefields live only in the distant memories of their families—they left no diaries or letters to remember them by. Many more died silently from disease and malnutrition—others from despair—in prisons like Andersonville, without leaving us a trace of their pain and suffering.

But those who survived and told us their tales left us a legacy—a quiet legacy of courage and determination that is not celebrated in speeches given at monuments honoring the dead, or at ceremonies awarding soldiers with Silver Stars or Purple Hearts. These are children speaking—in simple words—without rhetoric or resentment—telling us about human resilience and the capacity for compassion and decency that survives even when the world is awash in armed conflicts and hate. Perhaps, just perhaps, there is a lesson there that the grown-ups need to learn, and that's why the lesson is repeated by the children of war in each generation, century after century. We need only to listen to their voices:

In August 1864, during the siege of Atlanta, Carrie Berry noted in her diary: "I was ten-years-old today. I did not have a cake. Times are too hard. . . . I hope that by my next birthday, we will have peace in our land."

One hundred and thirty years later, in 1994, during the siege of Sarajevo, thirteen-year-old Neruia wrote a letter "To my unknown American Friend": "I love my country but now there is war here. Every day life is dangerous. Lots of young people lost legs and our hospitals are full. A lot of shells fall in my street. I want peace. I want the shells not to fall on my city, I want that the people not perish on the streets."

In November 1996, a young Vietnamese woman laid a wreath at the Vietnam War Memorial in Washington, D.C., in a gesture of forgiveness.[11] When she was nine years old, her small body had been badly burned by napalm in an air attack ordered by an American commander in the central highlands of Vietnam. The photo of the little girl, running naked along a country road, arms outstretched, screaming in agony and terror, became one of the most painful images of that war. Said Phan Thi Kim Phuc about the tragedy that befell her: "I have suffered a lot from both physical and emotional pain. . . . But God saved my life and gave me faith and hope. . . . We cannot change history, but we should try to do good things for the present and the future."

Carrie Berry from Atlanta, Naruia and Zlata from Sarajevo, and Phan Thi Kim Phuc from Vietnam never met in real life. They lived on three different continents, centuries apart. But they have a lot in common: They were children who loved life. They were not bitter; they did not hate. The wars that shaped their lives were fought in the name of causes that adults believed in and were willing to kill for. Many children died as well. These young girls survived, hoping, against all odds, that some day there might be the possibility of peace.

SELECT CHRONOLOGY
OF THE CIVIL WAR

The events listed below provide context for the eyewitness accounts related in this book.

1861

April 12	War begins with Confederate bombardment of Fort Sumter.
April 15	President Lincoln calls for 75,000 militia volunteers to serve for three months.
April 18	Federals abandon arsenal at Harpers Ferry, Virginia.
July 21	First battle of Bull Run (or Manassas), Virginia. Confederate victory.
August 29	Fort Hatteras, North Carolina, captured by Federals.
November 7	Union forces capture Port Royal, South Carolina.

1862

February 6	Fort Henry, Tennessee, falls to Union gunboats.
February 16	General Grant obtains unconditional surrender at Fort Donelson, Tennessee.
April 6–7	Battle of Shiloh (or Pittsburg Landing), Tennessee. Union victory.
April 25	New Orleans, Louisiana, captured by Federal fleet under David Farragut.
June 1	General Lee placed in command of Army of Northern Virginia.
June 6	Federal forces capture Memphis, Tennessee.
August 6	Baton Rouge bombarded; one-third of city destroyed.
August 29–30	Second battle of Bull Run (or Manassas), Virginia. Confederate victory.
September 4	Lee begins crossing Potomac into Maryland.
September 17	Battle of Antietam (or Sharpsburg), Maryland. Union victory.
September 22	Lincoln issues preliminary Emancipation Proclamation.
December 13	Battle of Fredericksburg, Virginia. Confederate victory.

1863

January 1	Emancipation Proclamation goes into effect.
April 16	Porter's fleet runs past batteries at Vicksburg, Mississippi.
May 1–4	Battle of Chancellorsville, Virginia. Confederate victory.
May 14	Grant captures Jackson, Mississippi's capital.
May 17	Confederate stand at Big Black River ends with rout.
May 18	Grant begins siege of Vicksburg.
June 3	Lee puts his army in motion for second invasion of the North.
July 1–3	Battle of Gettysburg, Pennsylvania. Union victory.
July 4	Vicksburg surrenders to Grant. Lee begins retreat to Virginia.
July 8	Port Hudson, Louisiana, capitulates.
September 19–20	Battle of Chickamauga, Georgia. Confederate victory.

1864

March 10	Grant made general-in-chief of Grand Armies of the United States.
May 7	Sherman begins drive toward Atlanta, Georgia.
June 18	Siege of Petersburg, Virginia, begins as Federal assaults fail.
July 17– September 1	Series of maneuvers, skirmishes, and battles for possession of Atlanta.
September 2	Atlanta falls to Sherman's army.
November 8	Lincoln elected to second term.
November 16	Sherman begins march to sea, leaving much of Atlanta in ruins.
November 22	Milledgeville, Georgia, occupied by troops under Sherman.
December 21	Sherman's army takes Savannah, Georgia.
December 22	Sherman offers Savannah to Lincoln as a Christmas gift.

1865

February 1	Sherman begins march through the Carolinas.
February 17	Columbia, South Carolina, ravaged by fire after falling to Sherman. Confederates evacuate Charleston.
March 11	Sherman takes Fayetteville, North Carolina.
March 29	Appomattox campaign begins with flanking movement by Federals.
April 2	Federals assault Petersburg defenses. Confederate government flees Richmond. Night finds city in flames. Lee begins retreat westward.
April 4–5	Lincoln visits Richmond.
April 6	Confederates defeated at Sayler's Creek.
April 9	Lee surrenders at Appomattox Court House. Lee's army being keystone of Confederacy, stage is set for general surrender of Southern forces.
April 14	Lincoln shot at Ford's Theater; dies the next morning.
May 23–24	Union armies parade in Washington prior to disbandment.

NOTES

Prologue

1. Anne Frank, *Diary of a Young Girl* (New York: Random House, 1952).

Epilogue

1. UNICEF's Fiftieth Anniversary Issue, *The State of the World's Children* (New York: Oxford University Press, 1996); Secretary General, United Nations, *Promotion and Protection of the Rights of Children: Impact of Armed Conflict on Children* (New York: United Nations General Assembly, 1996).

2. Roger Rosenblatt, *Children of War* (New York: Anchor Press, 1983).

3. Human Rights Watch Children's Rights Project, *Children in Combat* (New York: Human Rights Watch, 1996).

4. "Dear Unknown Friend: Children's Letters from Sarajevo" (New York: Soros Foundation, 1995); Zlata Filipovic, *A Child's Diary from Sarajevo* (New York: Viking Press, 1994); and UNICEF, *I Dream of Peace* (New York: HarperCollins, 1994).

5. Naomi Richman, "Children in situations of political violence," *Journal of Child Psychology and Psychiatry*, 34 (1993): 1286–1302.

6. Erin Burnette, "Research looks at how children fare at times of war," *APA Monitor* (January 1996).

7. Kati David, *A Child's War: World War II Through the Eyes of Children* (New York: Avon Books, 1989).

8. Emmy E. Werner, "Resilience in Development," *Current Directions in Psychological Science*, 4 (1995): 81–85.

9. Sarah Moskovitz, *Love Despite Hate: Child Survivors of the Holocaust and Their Adult Lives* (New York: Schocken Books, 1983).

10. Mando Dalianis-Karambatzakis, *Early Trauma and Adult Resiliency: A Mid-Life Follow-up Study of Young Children Whose Mothers Were Political Prisoners During the Greek Civil War* (Stockholm: Karolinska Institute, 1994).

11. Elaine Scilonia, "A Painful Road from Vietnam to Forgiveness," *New York Times*, November 12, 1996.

BIBLIOGRAPHY

Alleman, Tillie Pierce. 1888. *At Gettysburg, or What a Girl Saw and Heard of the Battle.* New York: W. Lake Borland.

Ambrose, Stephen E., ed. 1961. *A Wisconsin Boy in Dixie: Civil War Letters of James K. Newton.* Madison, Wis.: University of Wisconsin Press.

Andrews, Eliza Frances. 1908. *The War-Time Journal of a Georgia Girl.* New York: D. Appleton and Company.

Anonymous. 1903. "A Southern woman's recollections." In Mrs. Thomas Taylor, ed., *South Carolina's Women in the Confederacy.* Columbia, S.C.: State Company.

Bacon, G. W., and Howland, E. W., eds. 1899. *Letters of a Family During the War for the Union, 1861–1865.* New Haven, Conn.: Privately printed.

Balfour, Emma. 1863. "Diary." Manuscript. Jackson, Miss.: Department of Archives and History.

Bardalglio, Peter. 1992. "The children of jubilee: African-American childhood in wartime." In Catherine Clinton and Nina Silber, eds., *Divided House: Gender and the Civil War.* New York: Oxford University Press.

Bardeen, Charles William. 1910. *A Little Fifer's War Diary.* Syracuse, N.Y.: C. W. Bardeen.

Bates, Ralph Orr. 1910. *Billy and Dick from Andersonville Prison to the White House.* Santa Cruz, Calif.: Press Sentinel.

Bayley, William Hamilton. 1903. " Stories of the battle." Typescript. Gettysburg, Penn.: Library of National Military Park. Originally published in *Gettysburg Compiler.*

Bell, L. McRae. 1912. "A girl's experience in Vicksburg." *Harper's Weekly* 56, June: 12–13.

Berlin, Ira, ed. 1982. "A brother's war: Black soldiers and their kinfolk." In *Freedom: A Documentary History of Emancipation: 1861–1867.* Series II, *The Black Military Experience.* New York: Cambridge University Press.

Berry, Carrie. "Diary: August 1864–January 1866." Civil War Manuscript 29f, Atlanta History Center Library/Archives, Atlanta, Ga.

Bircher, William. 1889. *A Drummer Boy's Diary: Comprising Four Years of Service with the Second Regiment Minnesota Veterans Volunteers: 1861–1865.* St. Paul, Minn.: St. Paul Book and Stationary Company.

Blocker, Albert S. 1978. "The boy bugler of the Third Texas cavalry." *Military History of Texas and the Southwest* 14 (2): 71–92.

Bradford, Susan Eppes. 1926. *Through Some Eventful Years.* Macon, Ga.: J. W. Burke Company.

Bremner, Robert H. 1970. *Children and Youth in America: A Documentary History: Vol. I, 1600–1865.* Cambridge, Mass.: Harvard University Press.

Broadhead, Sarah M. 1863. *The Diary of a Lady of Gettysburg, Pennsylvania, from June 15 to July 15.* Unpublished Manuscript (copies available at Gettysburg National Military Park bookstore).

Brock, Sallie A. 1867. *Richmond During the War: Four Years of Personal Observations by a Richmond Lady.* New York: Carlton.

Burge, Dolly Summer (Lunt). 1927. *A Woman's Wartime Journal.* Macon, Ga.: J. W. Burke Company.

Cable, George W., ed. 1889. "The war diary of a Union woman in the South." *The Century Magazine* 38, October: 931–946.

Campbell, Henry. 1965. "Skirmishing in East Tennessee, the Atlanta and Nashville campaigns, end of the war and home." *Civil War Times Illustrated* 3, January: 36–39.

Century Magazine, ed. 1894. *The Century War Book: The Famous History of the Civil War by the People Who Actually Fought It.* New York.

Chancellor, Sue M. 1968. "Personal recollections of the battle of Chancellorsville." *Register of the Kentucky Historical Society* 66, April: 137–146.

Clem, John L. 1914. "From nursery to battlefield." *Outlook* 57: 546–547.

Commanger, Henry Steele. 1950. *The Blue and the Gray: The Story of the Civil War as Told by Participants.* Vol. 1: *The Nomination of Lincoln to the Eve of Gettysburg;* and Vol. 2: *The Battle of Gettysburg to Appomattox.* Indianapolis, Ind.: Bobbs-Merrill.

Cooke, Chauncy H. 1920/21. "A soldier boy's letters to his father and mother." *Wisconsin Magazine of History* 4: 75–100.

Cotton, Gordon A. 1989. *Yankee Bullets, Rebel Rations.* Vicksburg, Miss.: Office Supply Company.

Daniels, Elizabeth. 1989. "The children of Gettysburg." *American Heritage,* May–June: 97–107.

Davis, Kenneth C. 1996. *Don't Know Much About the Civil War.* New York: William Morrow and Company.

Davis, Varinna Howell. 1890. *Jefferson Davis: A Memoir by His Wife.* New York: The Bradford Company.

Dougherty, Michael. 1908. *Prison Diary of Michael Dougherty, Late Co. B. 13th Pennsylvania Cavalry, Sole Survivor of 127 of His Regiment.* Bristol, Penn.: C. A. Dougherty.

Drake, George. 1964. *The Mail Goes Through, or the Civil War Letters of George Drake: Over 80 Letters Written from August 9, 1862, to May 29, 1865.* Compiled and edited by Julia A. Drake. San Angelo, Tex.: Anchor Publishing Company.

Early, John Cabell. 1970. "A Southern boy at Gettysburg." *Civil War Times Illustrated* 9, June: 35–41.

Fleet, Benjamin Robert. 1962. *Green Mount: A Virginia Plantation Family During the Civil War: Being the Journal of Benjamin Robert Fleet and Letters of His Family.* Betsy Fleet and John D.P. Fuller, eds. Lexington, Ky.: University of Kentucky Press.

Foote, Corydon Edward. 1960. *With Sherman to the Sea: A Drummer's Story of the Civil War, as Related by Corydon Edward Foote to Olive Deane Hormel.* New York: John Day Company.

Foote, Shelby. *The Civil War: A Narrative.* Vol. 1 (1958): *Fort Sumter to Perryville;* Vol. 2 (1963): *Fredericksburg to Meridian;* Vol. 3 (1974): *Red River to Appomattox.* New York: Random House.

Forten, Charlotte. 1953. *The Journal of Charlotte L. Forten.* Ray Allen Billington, ed. New York: Collier Books.

Galwey, Thomas Francis. 1961. *The Valiant Hours: Narrative of "Captain Brevet," an Irish-American in the Army of the Potomac.* W. S. Nye, ed. Harrisburg, Penn.: Stockpole Press.

Garcia, Céline Frémaux. 1987. *Céline Remembering Louisiana: 1850–1871.* Athens, Ga.: University of Georgia Press.

Gay, Mary A. 1897. *Life in Dixie During the War.* Atlanta, Ga.: Charles P. Byrd.

Gerrish, Theodore. 1882. *Army Life: A Private's Reminiscences of the Civil War.* Portland, Me.: Hoyt, Fogg and Donham.

Gibbs, George Alphonso. 1965. "With a Mississippi private in a little known part of the battle of the first Bull Run and at Ball's Bluff." *Civil War Times Illustrated* 4, April: 42–47.

Gilmer, Loulie. 1862. "Letter to her father, March 16." Gilmer Papers, Southern Historical Collection, Chapel Hill, N.C.: University of North Carolina.

Goddard, Charles E. 1861. "Letter to his mother, December 2." Manuscript. St. Paul, Minn.: Minnesota Historical Society.

Gordon, Eleanor K. 1964. "Reminiscences of Sherman's visit to Savannah." In Katherine M. Jones, ed., *When Sherman Came: Southern Women and "the Great March,"* Indianapolis, Ind.: Bobbs-Merrill.

Grant, Frederick Dent. 1887. "At the front with Dad." *National Tribune,* reprinted in *Literary Digest,* April 27, 1912.

Harris, Leroy W. 1940. *Reminiscences of Confederate Soldiers,* Vol. 9. Atlanta: Georgia Department of Archives and History.

Hawthorne, Sally. 1964. "Memoirs." In Katherine M. Jones, ed., *When Sherman Came: Southern Women and "the Great March,"* Indianapolis, Ind.: Bobbs-Merrill.

Helper, Hinton R. 1857. *The Impending Crisis of the South.* New York: Burdick Brothers.

Higginson, Thomas Wentworth. 1870. *Army Life in a Black Regiment.* Boston: Fields, Osgood and Company.

Hollinger, Liberty Ann. 1938. "The battle of Gettysburg." *Journal of Pennsylvania History* 5, July: 66–78.

Hunt, Frances Caldern de la Barca. 1974. "The last days of Richmond." *Civil War Times Illustrated* 12, February: 20–22.

Jackson, Mattie J. 1866. *The Story of Mattie J. Jackson.* Lawrence, Kan.: Sentinel Office, 123 Essex Street.

Jones, Katherine M. 1955. *Heroines of Dixie: Confederate Women Tell Their Story of the War.* Indianapolis, Ind.: Bobbs-Merrill.

Jones, Katherine M. 1964. *When Sherman Came: Southern Women and "the Great March."* Indianapolis, Ind.: Bobbs-Merrill.

Josephy, Alvin M. Jr. 1991. *The Civil War in the American West.* New York: Alfred A. Knopf.

Kieffer, Henry Martin. 1889. *The Recollections of a Drummer Boy.* Boston: Ticknor and Company.

Lane, Mills, ed. 1977. *Dear Mother, Don't Grieve About Me: If I Get Killed, I'll Only Be Dead: Letters from Georgia Soldiers in the Civil War*. Savannah, Ga.: Beehive Press.

Leaphart, Mary Janney. 1885. "Experiences during the Civil War." In Allie Travis, ed. *Our Women in the War: the Lives they Lived; the Deaths They Died*. Charleston, SC: The News and Courier Book Presses.

LeConte, Emma. 1957. *When the World Ended: The Diary of Emma LeConte*. Earl Schenck Miers, ed. New York: Oxford University Press; reprint, Lincoln, Nebr.: University of Nebraska Press, 1987.

Lewis, Andrew. 1977. "The Civil War letters of Captain Andrew Lewis and his daughter." Michael Barton, ed. *Western Pennsylvania Historical Magazine* 60, October: 371–380.

L.F.J. 1885. "Child Wife of 1863." In Allie Travis, ed., *Our Women in the War: The Lives They Lived; the Deaths They Died*. Charleston, S.C.: The News and Courier Book Presses.

Litwack, Leon F. 1979. *Been in the Storm So Long: The Aftermath of Slavery*. New York: Alfred A. Knopf.

Lockwood, James D. 1893. *Life and Adventures of a Drummer Boy, or Seven Years a Soldier*. Albany, N.Y.: John Skinner.

Lord, Mrs. W. W. 1863. "Diary of a woman during the siege of Vicksburg." Manuscript #555, Civil War Manuscript Collection, Washington, D.C.: Library of Congress.

Lord, William W. Jr. 1908. "A child at the siege of Vicksburg." *Harper's Monthly Magazine*, December: 44–53.

Loughborough, Mary Ann. 1864. *My Cave Life in Vicksburg*. New York: Appleton and Company.

Marmion, Anne. 1959. *Under Fire: An Experience in the Civil War*. Compiled and edited by William Vincent Marmion Jr. Privately printed.

Martin, Robert Hugh. 1977. *A Boy of Old Shenandoah*. Caroline Martin Rutherford, ed. Parson, W. Va.: McClain Printing Company.

Maury, Betty Herndon. 1938. *The Confederate Diary of Betty Herndon Maury, Daughter of Lt. Commander M. F. Maury: 1861–1863*. Alice Maury Parmelee, ed. Washington, D.C.: Privately printed.

McCarthy, Cariton. 1882. *Detailed Minutia of Soldier Life in the Army of Northern Virginia, 1861–1865*. Richmond, Va.: C. McCarthy and Company.

McCreary, Albertus. 1909. "Gettysburg: A Boy's Experience of the Battle." *McClure's Magazine* 33, May–October: 243–253.

McCurdy, Charles. 1929. *Gettysburg: A Memoir*. Pittsburgh: Read & Whitting Company.

McElroy, John. 1879. *Andersonville: A Story of Rebel Military Prison*. Toledo, Ohio: D. R. Locke.

McGuire, Judith. 1867. *Diary of a Southern Refugee During the War*. New York: Hale and Son.

Mettger, Zak. 1994. *Till Victory Is Won: Black Soldiers in the Civil War*. New York: Lodestar Books.

Moore, Marinda Branson. 1863. *Geographical Reader for the Dixie Children*. Raleigh, N.C.: Branson, Farrar and Company.

Moskow, Shirley Blotnick. 1990. *Emma's World: An Intimate Look at Lives Touched by the Civil War*. Far Hills, N.J.: New Horizon Press.

Murphy, Jim. 1990. *The Boy's War: Confederate and Union Soldiers Talk About the Civil War*. New York: Clarion Books.

_____. 1992. *The Long Road to Gettysburg*. New York: Clarion Books.

Patterson, Josiah. 1861. "Letter to his dear little sons, December 18." Reprinted in Mills Lane, ed., *Dear Mother, Don't Grieve About Me: If I Get Killed, I'll Only Be Dead: Letters from Georgia Soldiers in the Civil War*. Savannah, Ga.: Beehive Press, 1977.

Rawick, George, ed. 1972. *The American Slave: A Composite Autobiography*. Series 1. Vols. 2 and 3, *South Carolina Narratives*; Vol. 6, *Alabama Narratives*; Vols. 8, 9, and 10, *Arkansas Narratives*; Vol. 13, *Georgia Narratives*; Vol. 14, *North Carolina Narratives*. Westport, Conn.: Greenwood Publishing Company.

Redkey, Edwin S., ed. 1992. *A Grand Army of Black Men: Letters from African-American Soldiers in the Union Army, 1861–1865*. New York: Cambridge University Press.

Reed, Lida Lord. 1901. "A woman's experience during the siege of Vicksburg." *The Century Magazine*, April: 922–928.

Reid, Harvey. 1862. "Letter to his brother Charles." Manuscript. Madison, Wis.: Wisconsin Historical Society.

Rooney, Henry Clay. 1979. "Reminiscences of the experiences of a boy soldier in the war between the states." *Richmond County History* 11, Winter: 20–25.

Rumph, Langdon Leslie. 1960. "Letters of a Teenage Confederate." *Florida Historical Quarterly* 38, April: 339–346.

Schiller, Herbert M., ed. 1994. *A Captain's War: The Letters and Diaries of William H.S. Burgwyn, 1861–1865*. Shippensburg, Penn.: White Mane Publisher.

Shay, R. E., ed. 1963. "Reflections on the battle of Gettysburg: A letter of Ms. Jeannie McCreary." *Journal of the Lebanon County Historical Society* 13: 278–284.

Sherman, W. T. 1909. *Home Letters of General Sherman*. New York: Charles Scribner's Sons.

Skelly, Annie M. 1941. "Remembrances of the battle of Gettysburg." Typescript. Gettysburg, Penn.: Adams County Historical Society.

Skelley, Daniel Alexander. 1932. *A Boy's Experiences During the Battle of Gettysburg*. Gettysburg, Penn.: Privately printed.

Smith, Jennie Pye. 1940. "When Sherman's raiders came." In Katherine M. Jones, ed., *When Sherman Came: Southern Women and "the Great March,"* Indianapolis, Ind.: Bobbs-Merrill, 1964.

Smith, William B. 1893. *On Wheels and How I Came There: A Real Story for Real Boys and Girls Giving the Personal Experiences and Observations of a Fifteen-year-Old Yankee Boy as a Soldier and Prisoner in the American Civil War*. New York: Hunt and Eaton.

Spangler, Edward Webster. 1904. *My Little War Experience: With Historical Sketches and Memorabilia*. York, Penn.: York Daily Publishers.

Stepto, Michele, ed. 1994. *Our Story, Our Toil: The Story of American Slavery as Told by Slaves*. Brookfield, Conn.: Millbrook Press.

Stockwell, Elisha. 1958. *Private Elisha Stockwell, Jr., Sees the Civil War*. Norman, Okla.: University of Oklahoma Press.

Straubing, Harold E., ed. 1985. *Civil War Eyewitness Reports*. Hamden, Conn.: Archon Books.

Taylor, Susie King. 1902. *Reminiscences of My Life in Camp with the 33rd United States Colored Troops*. Boston: Privately printed; reprint, New York: Marcus Wiener Publishing Company, 1988.

Tunnard, William H. 1866. *A Southern Record: The History of the Third Regiment Louisiana Infantry*. Baton Rouge, La.: Privately printed.

United States Congress. 1865. Joint Committee on the Conduct of the War, Second Session, 38th Congress. "Massacre of Cheyenne Indians," III–IV. Washington, D.C.: Government Printing Office.

United States War Department. 1865. "The Trial of Captain Henry Wirz." *Adjudant General's Office, Official Records*. Washington, D.C.: Government Printing Office.

Upson, Theodore Frelinghuysen. 1943. *With Sherman to the Sea: The Civil War Letters, Diaries, and Reminiscences of Theodore F. Upson*. Oscar Osburn Winther, ed. Baton Rouge, La.: Louisiana State University Press; reprint, Bloomington, Ind.: Indiana University Press, 1958.

Walker, Peter F. 1960. *Vicksburg: A People at War: 1861–1865*. Chapel Hill, N.C.: University of North Carolina Press.

Wallace, Kate Darling. 1983. *Child of Glencoe: Civil War Journal of Katie Darling Wallace*. Eleanor P. Cross and C. B. Cross Jr., eds. Chesapeake, Va.: Norfolk County Historical Society.

Ward, Evelyn Douglas. 1978. *The Children of Bladensfield*. New York: Viking Press.

Ward, G. C., ed. 1990. *The Civil War: An Illustrated History*. New York: Alfred A. Knopf.

Warren, Leander H. 1926. *My Recollections of What I Saw Before, During and After the Battle of Gettysburg*. Gettysburg, Penn.: Battlefield Press.

Washington, Booker T. 1905. *Up, from Slavery: An Autobiography*. New York: Doubleday, Page and Company.

Wheeler, Richard. 1978. *The Siege of Vicksburg*. New York: Thomas Crowell.

_____. 1978. *Sherman's March*. New York: Thomas Crowell.

_____. 1987. *Witness to Gettysburg*. New York: Harper and Row.

Wiley, Bell Irvin. 1943. *The Life of Johnny Reb, the Common Soldier of the Confederacy*. Indianapolis, Ind.: Bobbs-Merrill.

_____. 1952. *The Life of Billy Yank, the Common Soldier of the Union*. Indianapolis, Ind.: Bobbs-Merrill.

Williams, Noble C. 1902. *Echoes from the Battlefield, or Southern Life During the War*. Atlanta, Ga.: Franklin Printing and Publishing Company.

Wise, John S. 1899. *The End of an Era*. New York: Houghton Mifflin and Company.

Woodward, C. Vann, ed. 1981. *Mary Chesnut's Civil War*. New Haven, Conn.: Yale University Press.

Young, Annie. 1863. "Letter to dearest Annie, July 5." Edward McPherson Papers, Box 48, 1863 Correspondence, Library of Congress, Washington, D. C.

_____. 1863. "Letter to dear Mina, July 17." Edward McPherson Papers, Box 48, 1863 Correspondence, Library of Congress, Washington, D.C.

Index